The Rites of Lucifer

On the altar of the Devil up is down, pleasure is pain, darkness is light, slavery is freedom, and madness is sanity. The Satanic ritual chamber is the ideal setting for the entertainment of unspoken thoughts or a veritable palace of perversity.

Now one of the Devil's most devoted disciples gives a detailed account of all the traditional Satanic rituals. Here are the actual texts of such forbidden rites as the Black Mass and Satanic Baptisms for both adults and children.

The Satanic Rituals
Anton Szandor LaVey

AVON BOOKS
An Imprint of HarperCollins*Publishers*

AVON BOOKS
An Imprint of HarperCollins*Publishers*
195 Broadway
New York, NY 10007

Copyright © 1972 by Anton LaVey
ISBN: 0-380-01392-4
www.avonbooks.com

First Avon Books printing: December 1972

Avon Trademark Reg. U.S. Pat. Off. and in Other Countries, Marca Registrada, Hecho en U.S.A.
HarperCollins® is a trademark of HarperCollins Publishers Inc.

Printed in the U.S.A.

60

The ultimate effect of shielding men from the effects of folly is to fill the world with fools.

—Herbert Spencer

— CONTENTS —

The Satanic Rituals

INTRODUCTION

The rituals contained herein represent a degree of candor not usually found in a magical curriculum. They all have one thing in common—homage to the elements truly representative of the *other side*.

The Devil and his works have long assumed many forms. Until recently, to Catholics, Protestants were devils. To Protestants, Catholics were devils. To both, Jews were devils. To the Oriental, the Westerner was a devil. To the American settler of the Old West, the Red Man was a devil. Man's ugly habit of elevating himself by defaming others is an unfortunate phenomenon, yet apparently necessary to his emotional well-being. Though these precepts are diminishing in power, to virtually everyone some group represents evil incarnate. Yet if a human being ever thinks that someone else considers him wrong, or evil, or expendable in the affairs of the world, that thought is quickly banished. Few wish to carry the stigma of villain.

But wait. We are experiencing one of those unique periods in history when the villain consistently becomes heroic. The cult of the anti-hero has exalted the rebel and the malefactor.

Because man does little in moderation, selective acceptance of new and revolutionary themes is nonexistent. Consequently all is chaos, and anything goes, however irrational, that is against established policy. Causes are a dime a dozen. Rebellion for rebellion's sake often takes precedent over genuine need for change. The opposite has become desirable, hence this becomes the Age of Satan.

11

Dire as this appears, yet when the dust of the battles settles what truly needed changing will have been changed. The sacrifices will have been offered, human and otherwise, so that long-range development might continue, and stability return. Such is the odyssey of the twentieth century. The acceleration of man's development has reached an epic point of change. The evasive theologies of the immediate past were necessary to sustain the human race while the higher man developed his dreams and materialized his plans, until the frozen sperm of his magical child could be born upon the earth. The child has emerged in the form of Satan—the opposite.

The cold and hungry of the past produced offspring to till the fields and work the mills. Their cold will stop and their hunger shall end, but they will produce fewer children, for the by-product of the magician's frozen seed which has been born upon the earth will perform the tasks of the human offspring of the past. Now it is the higher man's role to produce the children of the future. Quality is now more important than quantity. One cherished child who can *create* will be more important than ten who can produce—or fifty who can *believe!* The existence of the man-god will be apparent to even the simplest, who will see the miracles of his creativity. The old belief that a supreme being created man and man's thinking brain will be recognized as an illogical sham.

It is altogether too easy to dismiss Satanism as a total invention of the Christian Church. It is said that the principles of Satanism did not exist before sectarian propaganda invented Satan. Historically, the word Satan did not have a villainous meaning before Christianity.

The "safe" schools of witchcraft, with their strict adherence to their horned-god-fertility-symbol syndrome, consider the words *Devil* and *Satan* anathema. They disclaim any association. They wish no comparisons to be drawn linking their Murrayite—Gardnerian—"neo-pagan"—"traditional" beliefs with Diabolism. They have expunged *Devil* and *Satan* from their vocabulary, and have waged a tireless campaign to give dignity to the word witch, though that has always been synonymous with nefarious activity, whether as witch, or hexe, or venifica, or other. They wholeheartedly *accept* the Christian evaluation of the word *Satan* at face value, and ignore the fact that the term became synonymous with evil simply because it was (a) of Hebrew origin, and anything Jewish was of the Devil, and (b) because it meant adversary or opposite.

With all the debate over the origin of the word witch, and the clear origins of the word Satan one would think that logic would rule, and Satan would be accepted as a more sensibly explained label.* Even if one recognizes the character inversion employed in changing Pan (the good guy) into Satan (the bad guy), why reject an old friend just because he bears a new name and unjustified stigma? Why do so many still feel it mandatory to disavow any connection with what might be classed as Satanic, yet increasingly use each and every one of the arts that were for centuries considered Satan's? Why does the scientist, whose academic and laboratory forebears suffered from accusations of heresy, mouth platitudes of Christian righteousness in one breath, while dismissing the concept of

---

*Controversy over the origin of the English word *witch* is valid when one considers the etymology of the term in other languages: *venifica* (Latin), *hexe* (German), *streghe* (Italian), etc. Only in its English form has the word assumed a benign origin: *wicca*, purportedly meaning "wise."

Any debate must center on recent claims that advance a positive and socially acceptable meaning for a term that has in all ages and most languages meant "poisoner," "frightener," "enchanter," "spell-caster," or "evil woman."

Anthropologists have shown that even in primitive societies, notably the Azande, the definition of *witch* carries malevolent connotations. Therefore, are we to assume that the only "good" witches in the world were English witches? This, however, becomes difficult to accept when one considers the term *wizard*, which stems from the Middle English *wysard* = *wise*, versus the Old English *wican* = *to bend*, from whence *witch* is supposedly derived. All in all, it seems to be an unsuccessful attempt to legitimatize a word that probably originated by onomatopoeia—the formation of a word that sounds like what it is intended to mean!

13

Satan in the next, when the man of science owes his heritage to what had for hundreds of years been relegated to Devildom?

The answers to these questions can be reduced to a single bitter charge: they cannot afford to admit to an affinity with anything that bears the name of Satan, for to do so would necessitate turning in their good-guy badges. What is even worse, the followers of the "Witchcraft-NOT-Satanism!" school harbor the same need to elevate themselves by denigrating others as do their Christian brethren, from whom they claim emancipation.

The rites in this book call the names of devils—devils of all shapes, sizes and inclinations. The names are used with deliberate and appreciative awareness, for if one can pull aside the curtain of fear and enter the Kingdom of Shadows, the eyes will soon become accustomed and many strange and wonderful truths will be seen.

If one is *truly* good inside he can call the names of the Gods of the Abyss with freedom from guilt and immunity from harm. The resultant feeling will be most gratifying. But there is no turning back. Here are the Rites of Lucifer . . . for those who dare remove their mantles of self-righteousness.

Anton Szandor LaVey
The Church of Satan
25 December VI Anno Satanas

CONCERNING THE RITUALS

Fantasy plays an important part in any religious curriculum, for the subjective mind is less discriminating about the quality of its food than it is about the taste. The religious rites of Satanism differ from those of other faiths in that fantasy is not employed to control the practitioners of the rites. The ingredients of Satanic ritual are not designed to hold the celebrant in thrall, but rather to serve his goals. Thus, fantasy is utilized as a magic weapon by the individual rather than by the system. This is not meant to imply that there are not, nor there will not exist, those who will claim dedication to Satanism as an *identity* while continuing to be manipulated unknowingly from without.

The essence of Satanic ritual, and Satanism itself, if taken up out of logic rather than desperation, is to objectively enter into a subjective state. It must be realized, however, that human behavior is almost totally motivated by subjective impulse. It is difficult therefore, to try to be objective once the emotions have established their preferences. Since man is the only animal who can lie to himself and believe it, he must consciously strive for some degree of self-awareness. Inasmuch as ritual magic is dependent upon emotional intensity for success, all manner of emotion producing devices must be employed in its practice.

The basic ingredients in the casting of a spell can be categorized as desire, timing, imagery, direction, and balance. Each of these is explained in the author's prior work, *The Satanic Bible*. The material contained in this volume represents the type of Satanic rite which has been employed in the past for specialized productive or destructive ends.

It will be observed that a pervasive element of paradox runs throughout the rituals contained herein. Up is down, pleasure is pain, darkness is light, slavery is freedom, madness is sanity, etc. In keeping with the very semantic and etymological meanings of Satan, situations, sensations and values are often inverted and reversed. This is not intended solely to serve as blasphemy—on the contrary, it is used to make it apparent that things are not always as they seem and that *no* standard can or should be deified, for under the proper conditions any standard can be changed.

Because Satanic Ritual so often exerts such change, both within the chamber and as an aftermath in the outside world, it is easy to assume that the upside-down cross and the Lord's Prayer recited backwards* usually linked with the *Black Mass* are also synonymous with Satanism. This generalization is correct in theory, since Satanism indeed represents the opposite viewpoint, and as such acts as a catalyst for change. The fact is, throughout history a "bad guy" has been needed so that those who are "right" can flourish. It was to be expected that the first *Messes Noirs* would institute reversals of existing liturgy, thus reinforcing the original blasphemy of heretical thought.

Modern Satanism realizes man's need for an "other side," and has realistically accepted that polarity—at least within the confines of a ritual chamber. Thus a Satanic chamber can serve —depending upon the degree of embellishment and the extent of the acts within—as a meditation chamber for the entertainment of unspoken thoughts, or a veritable palace of perversity.

Ceremonies such as the German *Wahsinn der Logisch* actually weld the concepts of Satanism and the manifestations of insanity into a total assumption of the role of needed social adversary. This phenomenon has been eloquently defined by

---

* Inaccurate assumption; the traditional *Messe Noir* employs a parody of *Matthew* 6:9 rather than a word-order inversion.

psychiatrist Thomas S. Szasz in *The Manufacture of Madness*.

Wherever this polarity of opposites exists, there is balance, life, and evolution. Where it is lacking, disintegration, extinction and decay ensue. It is high time that people learned that without opposites, vitality wanes. Yet *opposite* has long been synonymous with *bad*. Despite the prevalence of adages like "Variety is the spice of life."—"It takes all kinds . . ."—"The grass is always greener . . ." many people still automatically condemn whatever is opposite as "evil."

Action and reaction, cause and effect, are the bases of everything in the known universe. Yet when automobiles are generally large, it is said "no one will ever drive a small car," or when hem lines go up, "they'll never wear long dresses again," etc. The mere fact that the smugness—and boredom—of the populace rests on the mantra, "It'll *never* happen!" indicates to the magician that he must avoid such thinking. In magic the unexpected occurs—with such regularity, in fact, that it is safe to say that *to dwell on anything too long is to consume it.*

Magic is a push/pull situation, like the universe itself. While one is pushing, he cannot pull. The purpose in ritual is to "push" the desired result within a unique span of time and space, then move away and "pull" *by divorcing oneself from all thoughts and related acts previously ritualized.*

The productions contained here fall into two distinct categories: *rituals*, which are directed towards a specific end that the performer desires; and *ceremonies*, which are pageants paying homage to or commemorating an event, aspect of life, admired personage, or declaration of faith. Generally, a ritual is used to *attain*, while a ceremony serves to *sustain*.

For example, the traditional *Black Mass* would incorrectly be considered a ceremony—a pageant of blasphemy. Actually it is usually entered into for a personal need to purge oneself, via overcompensation, of inhibiting guilts imposed by Christian dogma. Thus it is a *ritual*. If a *Black Mass* is performed by curiosity seekers or "for fun," it becomes a party.

What constitutes the difference between a Satanic ceremony and a play presented by a theatre group? Often very little: mainly it hinges on the degree of acceptance on the part of the audience. It is of little consequence whether an outside audience does or does not accept the substance of a Satanic ceremony: the strange and grotesque always has a large and enthusiastic audience. Murders sell more newspapers than garden-club meetings. However, it is important to consider the needs of the participants: those who need Satanic ceremony most are the least likely to let themselves go before an audience of the curious.

Unlike encounter groups, the purpose of most Satanic ceremonies is to *elevate* the self rather than *demean* it. Encounter "therapy" is founded on the premise that if one is reduced in stature by another, who in turn has been reduced, all will have a firm foundation upon which to build. In theory this is admirable, for those who prefer to have *someone else* insult and browbeat them. They attain thereby a rather dubious form of recognition. For the masochistically inclined, encounter groups do provide a source of punishment and recognition. But what of those who have established an identity, those who are winners in the world, and have pride and rational self-interest, yet who possess the desire to express unpopular thoughts?

A ceremonial chamber essentially provides a stage for a performer who wishes complete acceptance from his audience. The audience becomes, in fact, part of the show. It has become fashionable in recent years to incorporate the audience into theatrical performances. This started with audience participation, with selected members of the audience called up to the stage to assist a performer in his role. Gradually this developed to such a degree that entire audiences mingled with the cast. Still, there can be no assurance that an audience will participate as a result of genuine enthusiasm, or merely because they are expected—or coerced—to do so.

A ceremony is dependent upon total single-mindedness of purpose on the part of *all* persons present. Even commemora-

18

tive pageants of a public nature suffer from divergence of thought and emotion during the festivities. A Fourth of July or Mardi Gras festival has a definite reason for its existence, yet how many participants maintain an awareness of its *raison d'être* while revelling? The festival becomes only an excuse, so to speak—a theme upon which to base social needs. Unfortunately, too many arcane and occult ceremonies and rituals wind up as just such excuses for social (and sexual) intercourse.

An important point to remember in the practice of any magic ritual or ceremony is: if you depend upon the activities within the chamber to provide or sustain a social climate, the ensuing energy—*conscious or otherwise*—directed toward these ends will *negate* any results you wish to obtain through the ritual! The line is fine between the desirability for close rapport between participants, and one's need *per se* for close rapport. The ritual will suffer if there is a single person in the chamber who drains the substance from it by his ulterior motives. Hence it is better to have three participants who are "with it" than twenty who *are* and three who *are not*. The most effective rituals are often the most solitary. This is why it is preposterous to attempt a ritual or ceremony with outsiders present who happen to be "sincerely interested" or "want to find out more about it" or "want to see what it's like."

A philosophical commitment is a prerequisite for acceptance into ritualistic activities, and this serves as a rudimentary screening process for organized Satanism. Consequently, a degree of compatibility—necessary to a successful working—exists within the chamber. Of course, anyone can say, "I believe," simply to gain access. It will be up to the discerning magician to determine actual sincerity. Because *Lesser Magic* is everyday magic, a finely attuned sense of discrimination is essential for all accomplishment. In addition, one of the most important "commandments" of Satanism is: *Satanism demands study—not worship!*

This book was, for the most part, written because the author believes that ritual magic should be removed from the sealed vacuum in which it has been held by occultists. Scant years ago, *The Satanic Bible* first publicly advanced magical techniques and working procedures utilizing sexual energy and other emotional responses. Since then many volumes have appeared that give identical principles, in both technical and esoteric jargon. It is expected that the precedent established by the present work will likewise "free" others to reveal "hidden mysteries."

Why, it will be asked, is it deemed feasible to make these rituals public knowledge? Primarily because the demand is great —not only from curiosity-seekers, but from those who thirst for more than what is offered by the recent outpourings of pseudo-Cabbalistic, crypto-Christian writing. Another reason for this book is that there are many recent awesome discoveries which give the sorcerer new tools with which to experiment. That is also why it is now "safe" to advance much of the present material.

A third reason, and perhaps the most important of all, is that magic—like life itself—produces what one puts into it. This principle can be observed in countless facets of human behavior. Human beings invariably treat things (property, other persons, etc.) with the same degree of respect with which they regard themselves. If one has little self-respect, no matter how much of a surface ego is present, one has little respect for anything else. This will lessen or negate ultimate success— magical or otherwise.

The difference between prayer and magic can be compared to the difference between applying for a loan and writing out a blank check for a desired amount. A man applying for a loan (prayer) may have nothing but a job as collateral and must keep working and pay interest, should the loan be granted. Otherwise he will wind up with bad credit (purgatory). The man (magician) who writes the desired amount on the blank check, assumes there will be delivery of the merchandise, and he pays no interest. He is indeed fortunate—*but* he had better have sufficient funds (magical qualities) to cover the amount written, or he may wind up in far worse straits, and have his creditors (demons) out looking for him.

Magic, like any other tool, requires a skilled hand. This does not mean that one need be a magician's magician or an advanced scholar of occult teachings. But it requires an application of principles—principles learned through study and experience. Life itself demands application of certain principles. If one's wattage (potential) is high, and the proper principles are applied, there is very little that cannot be accomplished. The more readily one can apply the principles needed to effect a proficiency in *Lesser Magic*, the greater one's chances of attainment through the use of *ritual*—or *ceremonial*—magic.

Satanic Ritual is a blend of Gnostic, Cabbalistic, Hermetic, and Masonic elements, incorporating nomenclature and vibratory words of power from virtually every mythos. Though the rituals in this book are representative of different nations, it will be easy to perceive a basic undercurrent through the cultural variants.

Two each of the rites are French and German, their preponderance accountable to the rich wealth of Satanic drama and liturgy produced by those countries. The British, although enamored of ghosts, hauntings, pixies, witches, and murder mysteries, have drawn most of their Satanic repertoire from European sources. Perhaps this is because a European Catholic who wanted to rebel became a Satanist: an Englishman who wanted to rebel became a Catholic—that was blasphemy enough! If most Americans' knowledge of Satanism is gleaned from the tabloid press and horror films, the average Briton can boast of "enlightenment" from the pens of three of their writers: Montague Summers, Dennis Wheatley and Rollo Ahmed. The notable British exceptions to what historian Elliot Rose terms the "anti-Sadducee" school of literary probing into Satanism, are that author's bold work, *A Razor for a Goat*; and Henry T. F. Rhodes' comprehensive study, *The Satanic Mass*.

Approximately half of the rites contained in this volume

can be performed by four or less persons, thereby eliminating problems or failures which can arise if quantity takes precedence over quality in the selection of *dramatis personae*. Where group solidarity and singleness of purpose exists, ceremonies such as *Das Tierdrama*, *Homage to Tchort* and *The Call to Cthulhu*, can be celebrated effectively by a larger number of participants.

For the most part, the rites should be begun and ended with the procedures standard to Satanic liturgy. These are presented in detail in *The Satanic Bible*, and are indicated wherever the term *standard sequence*, or *customary manner* (or the equivalent), appears in the present text. Accouterments necessary to all rites, as well as the *Enochian Calls*, are likewise given in the *Bible*.

As to the pronunciation of the names involved (despite some occultists who insist, "You can't expect help from the forces you call upon if you can't pronounce their names right,"), assume that the forces, demons, or elementals have enough insight to judge a caller's worthiness on more profound criteria than his glib tongue or expensive shoes. Pronounce the names as they sound best to *you*, but don't assume that you have the *correct* pronunciation, exclusive of all others. The "vibratory" rate of the names is only as effective as your own ability to "vibrate" while saying them, neither of which terms is to be confused with *vibrato*.

The success of magical operations is dependent upon *application of principles* learned rather than the amount of data collected. This rule must be stressed, for ignorance of this fact is the one most consistent cause of magical incompetency—and the least likely to be considered as the reason for failure. The most successful individuals throughout history have been the people who learn a few good tricks and apply them well, rather than those with a whole bag full who don't know which trick to pull out at the right time—or how to use it once they get it out!

Much magical curricula is padded beyond belief with pseudo-esoteric data, the purpose of which is: (a) to make it tougher to learn, since no one places any credence in what comes too easy (though they constantly seek shortcuts, giveaways and miracles); (b) to provide many things that can go wrong, so that if a ritual doesn't work it can be said that the student was delinquent in his studies; (c) to discourage all but the most idle, bored, talentless, and barren (translation = introspective, mystical, spiritual) persons. Contrary to popular assumption, esoteric doctrines do not discourage nonachievers but actually encourage them to dwell in loftier ivory towers. Those with the greatest degree of *natural* magical ability are often far too busy with other activities to learn the "finer" points of the *Sephiroth, Tarot, I Ching,* etc.

This is not intended to suggest that there is no value in arcane wisdom. But, just because one memorizes every name in a telephone directory it does not mean he is intimately acquainted with each person listed.

It is often said that magic is an impersonal tool and therefore neither "white" nor "black," but creative or destructive, depending upon the magician. This implies that—like a gun— magic is as good or bad as its user's motivations. This, unfortunately, is a half-truth. It presumes that once a magician activates his magical weapon it will serve him according to his own propensities.

If a magician were dealing with only two elements—himself and his magical force—this theory could be valid. But under most circumstances, human actions and events are influenced and carried out by other human beings. If a magician wants to effect a change according to his will (personal) and employs magic as a tool (impersonal), he must often rely on a human vehicle (personal) to carry out his will. No matter how impersonal a force magic is, the emotional and behavioral pattern of the human vehicle must be considered.

It is too often assumed that if a magician curses someone the victim will meet with an accident or fall ill. This is an oversimplification. Often the most profound magical workings are those which engage the assistance of other unknown human

23

beings in order to effect the magician's will. A magician's destructive wish toward another may be justified by all laws of natural ethic and fair play, but the force that he summons may be wielded by a mean, worthless person—one whom the magician himself would despise—in order to complete the working. Oddly enough, this manner of operations can be employed for benevolent or amorous—rather than destructive—ends with equal success.

The Satanic Bible states that the magician should treat the entities he calls upon as friends and companions, for even an "impersonal" device will respond better to a conscientious and respectful user. This principle is accurate for operating automobiles and power tools, as well as demons and elementals.

It will be apparent to some readers that Satanic rites of the type contained in this book can act as catalysts for the actions of great numbers of people, and indeed they *have*—acting, in the words of Lovecraft, as the mind that is held by no head.

Whenever reference in this book is made to a priest, the role may also be taken by a woman who can serve in the capacity of priestess. It must be clarified, however, that the essence of Satanism—its dualistic principle—necessarily imposes an active/passive dichotomy upon the respective roles of celebrant and altar. If a woman serves as a celebrant, then for all intents and purposes she represents the masculine principle in the rite.

The pervasive theme of active/passive (Yin/Yang) in human relations cannot be stifled, despite attempts to create matriarchal, patriarchal, or unisexual societies. There will always be those who "might as well be men" or "might as well be women," depending upon their endocrinological, emotional and/or behavioral predilections. It is far sounder, from a magical standpoint, for an ego-driven or forceful woman to conduct a ritual, rather than a shy, introspective man. It might prove awkward, however, to cast a passive man in the role of Earth-Mother—as the altar—unless his appearance conveyed the image of a woman.

An exclusively homosexual group can often conduct more

fruitful rituals than a group with both heterosexual and homosexual participants. The reason is that each person in an all-homophile group is usually more aware of the individual active/passive propensities of his associates, and this ensures accurate role casting. It must be stressed that both male and female principles *must* be present, even if the *same* sex portrays both.

With few exceptions the rituals and ceremonies in this book have been written to meet existing conditions and requirements. Because a workable format depends on fairly recent standards of language, readily-understandable rubrics and emotion-producing litany cannot be set down without a certain degree of "Satanic license." There are virtually no Satanic rites over one hundred years old that elicit sufficient emotional response from today's practitioner, if the rites are presented in their original form. When the rites were initially conceived, they were amply provocative to the wizards who practiced them, of course. In short, one no longer reads a Victorian romance for sexual titillation.

No single element of a magical rite is quite as important as the words which are spoken, and unless the litany of a ritual is stimulating to the speaker, silence is far more desirable. The celebrant or priest conducting a rite must serve as a sounding board for the emotions of those in attendance. Through the strength of his words, his listeners' potential charge of magical energy can be inspired to peak intensity or wane to lethargy out of sheer boredom. However, many people are bored by *any* litany, no matter how meaningful or eloquent, so it behooves the magician to select his co-workers with care. Those who are perennially bored are usually stupid, insensitive, unimaginative individuals. They are deadwood in any ritual chamber.

Naturally, there is a reasonable level of possible emotional response which must be understood when selecting a litany to be used for ceremonial purposes. A wizard or cultist of 1800 may have thrilled at his words when speaking of "waiting at the darkness visible, lifting our eyes to that bright Morning Star, whose rising brings peace and salvation to the faithful and obedient of the human race." Now he may say, "standing at the gates of Hell to summon Lucifer, that he might rise and show himself as the harbinger of balance and truth to a world grown heavy with the spawn of holy lies," in order to engender the same emotional response.

The guiding thoughts behind Satanic rituals past and present have emanated from diverse minds and places, yet all operate on much the same "frequency." Many people who never conceptualized their personal philosophies discover that the principles of Satanism are an unequalled vehicle for their thoughts; hence the title of "Satanist" is now being claimed by its rightful owners. Those who disagree with the non-Christian definition of *Satanist*, as set forth in *The Satanic Bible*, should examine the basis of that disagreement. It surely stems from one of two sources: "common knowledge" or scripturally founded propaganda.

"Satan has been the best friend the church has ever had, as he has kept it in business all these years!"—the Ninth Satanic Statement—is not limited just to the religious organization referred to as "the church." How convenient an enemy the Devil has been for the weak and insecure! Crusaders against the Devil maintained that Satan, even if accepted on an anthropomorphic basis, was *neither so evil nor so dangerous that he could not be personally vanquished*. And so Satan has existed as a convenient enemy to be employed when needed—one who could be beaten by any lily-livered popinjay who could find the time to arm himself with a barrage of scriptural rhetoric! Thus Satan has made cowards into heroes, weaklings into gladiators, and wretches into nobles. That was so simply because his adversaries were able to tailor the rules of the game to suit their own needs. Now that there are *avowed* Satanists, who make *their* own standards, the rules of the game change. If a substance is harmful, its poisonous effects will speak for it. If Satanists are powerfully evil, then their foes have valid fears.

The "godly," have toughened Satan in his role of scapegoat,

while keeping him nourished and handy for their needs. Now it is *they* who have weakened and atrophied while Satan breaks his bonds. Now Satan's people can speak for Him, and they have a weapon calculated to annihilate the feeble and insipid mouthings of the pulpit pounders of the past. That weapon is logic.

The Satanist can easily invent fairy tales to match anything contained in holy writ, for his background is the very childhood of fiction—the myths immemorial of all peoples and all nations. And he admits they are fairy tales. The Christian cannot—no, *dares* not—admit that his heritage is fairy tales, yet he depends on them for his pious sustenance. The Satanist maintains a storehouse of *avowed* fantasy gathered from all cultures and from all ages. With his unfettered access to logic as well, he now becomes a powerful adversary of Satan's past tormentors.

Those who have depended on fighting the Devil to display their "goodness" must discover a new adversary—one who is helpless, disorganized, and easily vanquished. But the world is changing fast and such a recruitment will prove difficult, . . . so difficult, in fact, that witch-hunters and devil finders may be forced to seek their quarry in the most impenetrable of jungles—themselves.

Note

In rituals where a foreign language is presented, the English translation usually follows after a brief space.

Wherever both languages are so presented, only *one* should be employed. To reiterate a statement in an alternate language breaks the flow of the original statement.

If the foreign text is used, the English translation should be studied beforehand, so the meaning of the foreign text will be fully understood.

LE MESSE NOIR

THE ORIGINAL PSYCHODRAMA

The *Black Mass* is a valid Satanic ceremony only if one feels the need to perform it. Historically, there is no ritual more closely linked with Satanism than the *Black Mass*. It has long been considered the principal elective of Satanists, who were assumed never to tire of trampling on crosses and of stealing unbaptized infants. If a Satanist had nothing else to do, and was independently wealthy, newer and more blasphemous versions of the *Messe Noir* would be invented in order to nourish his jaded existence, the theory went. Though a titillating concept to many, it is without validity, and as devoid of logic as the assumption that Christians celebrate Good Friday every Wednesday afternoon.

Although the *Black Mass* is a ritual that has been performed countless times, the participants often were not Satanists, but would act solely on the idea that anything contradictory to God must be of the Devil. During the Inquisition, anyone who doubted the sovereignty of God and Christ was summarily considered a servant of Satan and suffered accordingly. The Inquisitors, needing an enemy, found one in the guise of witches who supposedly were subject to Satanic control. Witches were created in wholesale lots by the church from the ranks of the senile, sexually promiscuous, feeble-minded, deformed, hysterical, and anyone who happened to be of non-Christian thought or background. There was only a minute percentage of actual healers and oracles. They were likewise persecuted.

There have been recent attempts to assess great numbers of "witches" of antiquity as rebels against the Christian Church who held Dianic "esbats" with furtive regularity. This presents a charming picture. But it is folly, because it bestows a degree of intellectual sophistication on people who were essentially ignorant, and who were willing to go along with whatever form of worship the opinion makers gave them.

At any rate, during the period when accounts of the *Black Mass* were employed as propaganda against "heretical" sects and orders, few cared about the finer points differentiating the witch from the Satanist. Both were as one in the eyes of the Inquisitors, although it is safe to say that unlike the majority who bore the label of witch, those who conducted themselves "Satanically" often earned their stigma. This is not meant to condone the actions of the Inquisitors against such freethinkers and rebels, but to concede that they were a very real threat to the holy fathers. Such men as Galileo and da Vinci, accused of traffic with the Devil, most certainly were Satanic in the sense that they expressed ideas and theories destined to break down the status quo.

The supposed high point of the *Black Mass,* alleged to be the offering to Satan of an unbaptized human child, was not quite the way the collectors of baptism fees gloatingly told it.

Catherine Deshayes, known as LaVoisin, was a seventeenth century French businesswoman who peddled drugs and performed abortions. LaVoisin arranged "rituals, charms and spells" for her clients, all of whom wished to retain the safety of the Church, but whose ineffectual prayers drove them to seek darker magic. This sort of desperate miracle seeking is as prevalent today as it was then. In the performance of one of her more popular productions, a clandestine, highly commercial inversion of the Catholic mass, LaVoisin provided "authenticity" by actually engaging willing Catholic priests as celebrants and sometimes using an aborted fetus as a human sacrifice.

(Records indicate that she performed over two hundred abortions.)

The priests who supposedly celebrated the *Black Mass* for her supplied the holy propagandists with more material. If ordained priests were occasionally prone to take part in heretical rites, it is understandable when one considers the social conditions at the time. For centuries in France many men became priests because they were from upper class families and the priesthood was *de rigeur* for at least one son of cultured or well-to-do parents. The first son became a military officer or politician, and the second was sent off to a religious order. So controversial was this arrangement that it produced a catch phrase: *"Le rouge et noir."*

If one of the young men happened to be of intellectual bent, which was often the case, the priesthood provided virtually the only access to libraries and avenues of higher learning. It was to be expected that the Hermetic principle of "as above, so below" and vice versa would apply to gifted and intelligent individuals. An inquiring, well-developed mind could often be dangerously skeptical and subsequently irreverent! Thus there was always a supply of "depraved" priests ready and willing to celebrate Satanic rites.

History has, in fact, produced entire sects and monastic orders that fell into humanistic and iconoclastic fever. Think about it; *you* personally may have known of a priest or minister who wasn't quite what he should have been . . . ! Today, of course, in Christianity's death throes, anything goes in the clergy, and priests once tortured and executed for "vile heresies" (Urban Grandier, for example) would seem like Boy Scouts by current standards of pastoral conduct. The seventeenth century priests who celebrated the *Black Mass* need not have been intrinsically evil: heretical, most certainly; perverse, definitely; but harmfully evil, probably not.

The exploits of LaVoisin, which have been recounted in such a sensational manner, if simplified reveal her as a beautician, midwife, lady pharmacist, abortionist, who had a flair for

33

theatrics. Nevertheless, LaVoisin gave the Church what it needed: a real honest-to-Satan Black Mass. She provided much substance for their anti-heretic propaganda machine. LaVoisin put the *Black Mass* on the map, so to speak, and so succeeded in working some very real magic—magic far more potent than the spells she concocted for her clients. She gave people an *idea*.

Those who leaned to the ideas expressed by LaVoisin's rites needed little encouragement to attempt to duplicate the rites. For those persons the *Black Mass* provided a setting for various degrees of perversity, ranging from harmless and/or productive psychodrama to actual heinous acts that would substantiate the chroniclers' wildest fantasies. Depending on individual predilection, those who received inspiration from the likes of LaVoisin could either effect a therapeutically valid form of rebellion, or fill the ranks of the "Christian Satanists" —miscreants who adopt Christian standards of Satanism. One fact is irrefutable: for every unborn baby offered up "in the name of Satan" during LaVoisin's clandestine playlets, countless thousands of *living* babies and small children have been slaughtered in wars fought in the name of Christ.

The *Black Mass* which follows is the version performed by the *Societé des Luciferiens* in late nineteenth and early twentieth century France. Obviously taken from prior *Messes Noir*, it also derives from the texts of the *Holy Bible*, the *Missale Romanum*, the work of Charles Baudelaire and Charles Marie-George Huysmans, and the records of Georges Legué. It is the most consistently Satanic version this author has encountered. While it maintains the degree of blasphemy necessary to make it effective psychodrama, it does not dwell on inversion purely for the sake of blasphemy, but elevates the concepts of Satanism to a noble and rational degree. This ritual is a psychodrama in the truest sense. Its prime purpose is to reduce or negate stigma acquired through past indoctrination. It is also a vehicle for retaliation against unjust acts perpetrated in the name of Christianity.

Perhaps the most potent sentence in the entire mass follows the desecration of the Host: "Vanish into the void of thy empty Heaven, for thou wert never, nor shalt thou ever be." The possibility that Christ was a total invention has occurred to investigators with increasing frequency. Many once existing social ramifications might have made this feasible. Perhaps the recent last ditch "Christ, the man" stand is an attempt to sustain a dying myth through use of a single reinforcing element—one with which all can identify—that shows him a fallible human being!

Requirements for Performance

Participants consist of a priest (celebrant), his immediate assistant (deacon), a secondary assistant (subdeacon), a nun, an altar, an illuminator who holds a lighted candle where needed for reading, a thurifer, a gong-striker, an additional attendant and the congregation.

Hooded black robes are worn by all participants except two: a woman dressed as a nun, wearing the customary habit and wimple, and the woman who serves as the altar, who is nude. The priest conducting the mass is known as the celebrant. Over his robe he wears a chasuble bearing a symbol of Satanism—the Sigil of Baphomet, inverted pentagram, inverted cross, symbol of brimstone or black pine cones. Though some versions of the *Black Mass* were performed in vestments consecrated by the Roman Catholic Church, records indicate that such garments were the exception rather than the rule. The authenticity of a consecrated host seems to have been far more important.

The woman who serves as the altar lies on the platform with her body at right angles to its length, her knees at its edge and widely parted. A pillow supports her head. Her arms are outstretched crosswise and each hand grasps a candleholder containing a black candle. When the celebrant is at the altar, he stands between the woman's knees.

The wall over the altar should bear the Sigil of Baphomet

or an inverted cross. If both are employed, the Sigil of Baphomet must take the uppermost or prominent position, the cross occupying the space between the lower halves of the altar's legs.

The chamber should either be draped in black or in some way approximate the atmosphere of a medieval or gothic chapel. Emphasis should be placed on starkness and austerity, rather than finery and glitter.

All implements standard to Satanic ritual are employed: bell, chalice, phallus, sword, gong, etc. (see *Satanic Bible* for descriptions and use). In addition a chamber pot, thurible (censer) and incense boat are used.

The chalice containing wine or liquor is placed between the altar's thighs, and on it is a paten holding a round wafer of turnip or of coarse black bread. The chalice and paten should be shrouded with a square black veil, preferably of the same fabric as the celebrant's chasuble. Immediately in front of the chalice is placed an aspergeant or phallus.

The ritual book is placed on a small stand or pillow so that it is on the celebrant's right when he faces the altar. The illuminator stands at the side of the altar near the ritual book. Opposite him, on the other side of the altar, stands the thurifer with a thurible that holds ignited charcoal. Next to him stands the attendant holding the boat of incense.

Music should be liturgical in mood, preferably played on the organ. The works of Bach, de Grigny, Scarlatti, Palestrina, Couperin, Marchand, Clerambault, Buxtehude and Franck are most appropriate.

LE MESSE NOIR

[When all are assembled the gong is sounded and the celebrant, with the deacon and subdeacon preceding him, enters and approaches the altar. They halt somewhat short of the altar, the deacon placing himself at the celebrant's left, the subdeacon at his right. The three make a profound bow before the altar and commence the ritual with the following verses and responses.]

CELEBRANT:

In nomine Magni Dei Nostri Satanas. Introibo ad altare Domini Inferi.

DEACON AND SUBDEACON:
Ad eum qui laefificat meum.

CELEBRANT:
Adjutorium nostrum in nomine Domini Inferi.

DEACON AND SUBDEACON:
Qui regit terram.

CELEBRANT:
Before the mighty and ineffable Prince of Darkness, and in the

presence of all the dread demons of the Pit, and this assembled company, I acknowledge and confess my past error.

Renouncing all past allegiances, I proclaim that Satan-Lucifer rules the earth, and I ratify and renew my promise to recognize and honor Him in all things, without reservation, desiring in return His manifold assistance in the successful completion of my endeavors and the fulfillment of my desires.

I call upon you, my Brother, to bear witness and to do likewise.

DEACON AND SUBDEACON:

Before the mighty and ineffable Prince of Darkness, and in the presence of all the dread demons of the Pit, and this assembled company, we acknowledge and confess our past error. Renouncing all past allegiances, we proclaim that Satan-Lucifer rules the earth, and we ratify and renew our promise to recognize and honor Him in all things, without reservation, desiring in return His manifold assistance in the successful completion of our endeavors and the fulfillment of our desires.

We call upon you, His liege-man and priest, to receive this pledge in His name.

CELEBRANT:

Domine Satanas, tu conversus vivificabis nos.

DEACON AND SUBDEACON:

Et plebs tua laetabitur in te.

CELEBRANT:

Ostende nobis, Domine Satanas, potentiam tuam.

DEACON AND SUBDEACON:

Et beneficium tuum da nobis.

CELEBRANT:
Domine Satanas, exaudi meam.

DEACON AND SUBDEACON:
Et clamor meus ad te veniat.

CELEBRANT:
Dominus Inferus vobiscum.

DEACON AND SUBDEACON:
Et cum tuo.

CELEBRANT:
Gloria Deo, Domino Inferi, et in terra vita hominibus fortibus. Laudamus te, benedicimus te, adoramus te, glorificamus te, gratias agimus tibi propter magnam potentiam tuam: Domine Satanas, Rex Inferus, Imperator omnipotens.

Offertory

[The chalice and paten, on which rests the wafer of turnip or coarse black bread, are uncovered by the celebrant. He takes the paten into both hands, and raises it to about breast level in an attitude of offering, and recites the offertory words.]

CELEBRANT:
Suscipe, Domine Satanas, hanc hostiam, quam ego dignus famulus tuus offero tibi, Deo meo vivo et vero, pro omnibus circumstantibus, sed et pro omnibus fidelibus famulis tuis: ut mihi et illis proficiat ad felicitatem in hanc vitam. Amen.

[Replacing the paten and wafer, and taking the chalice into his hands, he raises it in like manner, reciting:]

CELEBRANT:

Offerimus tibi, Domine Satanas, calicem voluptatis carnis, ut in conspectu majestatis tuae, pro nostra utilitate et felicitate, placeat tibi. Amen.

[He replaces the chalice upon the altar and then, with hands extended, palms downward, recites the following:]

CELEBRANT:

Come, O Mighty Lord of Darkness, and look favorably on this sacrifice which we have prepared in thy name.

[The thurible and incense boat are then brought forward and the celebrant thrice sprinkles incense upon the burning coals while reciting the following:]

CELEBRANT:

Incensum istud ascendat ad te, Domine Inferus, et descendat super nos beneficium tuum.

[The celebrant then takes the thurible and proceeds to incense the altar and the gifts. First he incenses the chalice and wafer with three counterclockwise strokes, after which he makes a profound bow. Then he raises the thurible three times to the Baphomet (or to the inverted cross), and bows again. Then, assisted by the deacon and subdeacon, he incenses the top of the altar, then the sides of the platform, if possible by circumambulation. The thurible is returned to the thurifer.]

CELEBRANT:
Dominus Inferus vobiscum.

DEACON AND SUBDEACON:
Et cum tuo.

CELEBRANT:
Sursum corda.

DEACON AND SUBDEACON:
Habemus ad Dominum Inferum.

CELEBRANT:
Gratias agamus Domino Infero Deo nostro.

DEACON AND SUBDEACON:
Dignum et justum est.

[The celebrant then raises his arms, palms downward, and says the following:]

CELEBRANT:
Vere clignum et justum est, nos tibi semper et ubique gratias agere: Domine, Rex Inferus, Imerator Mundi. Omnes exercitus inferi te laudant cum quibus et nostras voces ut admitti jubeas deprecamur, dicentes:

[celebrant bows and says:]

Salve! Salve! Salve!

[gong is struck thrice]

41

Dominus Satanas Deus Potentiae. Pleni sunt terra et inferi gloria. Hosanna in excelsis.

The Canon

CELEBRANT:

Therefore, O mighty and terrible Lord of Darkness, we entreat You that You receive and accept this sacrifice, which we offer to You on behalf of this assembled company, upon whom You have set Your mark, that You may make us prosper in fullness and length of life, under Thy protection, and may cause to go forth at our bidding Thy dreadful minions, for the fulfillment of our desires and the destruction of our enemies. In concert this night we ask Thy unfailing assistance in this particular need. (Here is mentioned the special purpose for which the mass is offered).

In the unity of unholy fellowship we praise and honor first Thee, Lucifer, Morning Star, and Beelzebub, Lord of Regeneration; then Belial, Prince of the Earth and Angel of Destruction; Leviathan, Beast of Revelation; Abaddon, Angel of the Bottomless Pit; and Asmodeus, Demon of Lust. We call upon the mighty names of Astaroth, Nergal and Behemoth, of Belphegor, Adramelech, and Baalberith, and of all the nameless and formless ones, the mighty and innumerable hosts of Hell, by whose assistance may we be strengthened in mind, body and will.

[The celebrant then extends his hands, palms downward, over the offerings on the altar and recites the following:]

[The gong is sounded]

CELEBRANT:

Hanc igitur oblationem servitutis nostrae sed et cunctae familiae tuae, quaesumus, Domine Satanas, ut placatus accipias; diesque nostros in felicitate disponas, et in electorum tuorum jubeas grege numerari. Shemhamforash!

CONGREGATION:

Shemhamforash!

CELEBRANT:

Enlightened Brother, we ask a blessing.

[The subdeacon brings forth the chamber pot and presents it to the nun, who has come forward. The nun lifts her habit and urinates into the font. As she passes water, the deacon addresses the congregation:]

DEACON:

She maketh the font resound with the tears of her mortification. The waters of her shame become a shower of blessing in the tabernacle of Satan, for that which hath been withheld pourest forth, and with it, her piety. The great Baphomet, who is in the midst of the throne, shall sustain her, for she is a living fountain of water.

[As the nun completes her urination, the deacon continues:]

DEACON:

And the Dark Lord shall wipe all tears from her eyes, for He said unto me: It is done. I am Alpha and Omega, the beginning and the end. I will give freely unto him that is athirst of the fountain of the water of life.

[The subdeacon removes the font from the nun and holds it before the deacon, who dips the aspergeant into the fluid. Then, holding the aspergeant against his own genitals, the deacon turns to each of the cardinal compass points, shaking the aspergeant twice at each point, and says:]

DEACON:

(facing south) In the name of Satan, we bless thee with this, the symbol of the rod of life.

(facing east) In the name of Satan, we bless thee with this, the symbol of the rod of life.

(facing north) In the name of Satan, we bless thee with this, the symbol of the rod of life.

(facing west) In the name of Satan, we bless thee with this, the symbol of the rod of life.

The Consecration

[The celebrant takes the wafer into his hands and, bending low over it, whispers the following words into it:]

CELEBRANT:

Hoc est corpus Jesu Christi.

[He raises the wafer, placing it between the exposed breasts of the altar, and then touching it to the vaginal area. The gong is struck. He replaces the wafer on the paten which rests on the altar platform. Taking the chalice into his hands, he bends low over it, as with the wafer, and whispers the following words into it:]

CELEBRANT:

Hic est calix voluptatis carnis.

[He then raises the chalice above his head, for all to see. The gong is struck, and the thurifer may incense it with three swings of the thurible. The chalice is then replaced, and the following is recited:]

CELEBRANT:

To us, Thy faithful children, O Infernal Lord, who glory in our iniquity and trust in Your boundless power and might, grant that we may be numbered among Thy chosen. It is ever through You that all gifts come to us; knowledge, power and wealth are Yours to bestow. Renouncing the spiritual paradise of the weak and lowly, we place our trust in Thee, the God of the Flesh, looking to the satisfaction of all our desires, and petitioning all fulfillment in the land of the living.

DEACON AND SUBDEACON:

Shemhamforash!

CELEBRANT:

Prompted by the precepts of the earth and the inclinations of the flesh, we make bold to say:

Our Father which art in Hell, hallowed be Thy name.

Thy kingdom is come, Thy will is done; on earth as it is in Hell!

We take this night our rightful due, and trespass not on paths of pain.

Lead us unto temptation, and deliver us from false piety, for Thine is the kingdom and the power and the glory forever!

DEACON AND SUBDEACON:

And let reason rule the earth.

CELEBRANT:

Deliver us, O Mighty Satan, from all past error and delusion,
that, having set our foot upon the Path of Darkness and
vowed ourselves to Thy service, we may not weaken in our re-
solve, but with Thy assistance, grow in wisdom and strength.

DEACON AND SUBDEACON:

Shemhamforash!

[Celebrant recites the *Fifth Enochian Key* from *The Satanic Bible*.]

The Repudiation and Denunciation

[The celebrant takes the wafer into his hands, extends it
before him, and turns to face the assembled company,
saying the following:]

CELEBRANT:

Ecce corpus Jesu Christi, Dominus Humilim et Rex Servorum.

[The celebrant raises the wafer to the Baphomet. He continues in great anger . . .]

CELEBRANT:

Et toi, toi, qu'en ma qualité de prêtre, je
force, que tu le veuilles ou non, à descendre
dans cette hostie, à t'incarner dans ce pain,
Jésus, artisan de supercheries, larron
d'hommages, voleur d'affection, écoute!
Depuis le jour où tu sortis des entrailles

ambassadrices d'une Vierge, tu as failli à
tes engagements, menti a tes promesses;
des siècles ont sangloté, en t'attendant, Dieu
fuyard, Dieu muer! Tu devais rédimer les
hommes et tu n'as rien racheté; tu devais
apparaitre dans ta gloire et tu t'endors! Va,
mens, dis au misérable qui t'appelle:
"Espère, patiente, souffre, l'hôpital des
âmes te recevra, les anges t'assisteront,
le Ciél s'ouvre"—Imposteur! tu sais bien
que les anges dégoûtés de ton inertie
s'éloignent!—Tu devais être le Truchement
de nos plaintes, le Chambellan de nos pleurs,
tu devais les introduire près du Père et tu ne
l'as point fait, parce que sans doute cette
intercession dérangeait ton sommeil
d'Eternité béate et repue!

Tu as oublié cette pauvreté que tu prêchais,
vassal énamouré des banques! Tu as vu
sous le pressoir de l'agio broyer les faibles,
tu as entendu les râles des timides perclus par
les famines, des femmes éventrées pour un peu
de pain et tu as fait répondre par la Chancellerie
de tes Simoniaques, par tes représentants de
commerce, par tes Papes, des excuses
dilatoires, des promesses évasives, Basochien
de sacristie, Dieu d'affaires!

Monstre, dont l'inconcevable férocité engendra
la vie et l'infliegea à des innocents que tu
oses concamner, au nom d'on ne sait quel
péché originel, que tu oses punir, en vertu
d'on ne sait quelles clauses, nous voudrions
pourtant bien te faire avouer enfin tes impu-
dents mensonges, tes inexpiables crimes!

Nous voudrions taper sur tes clous, appuyer sur tes épines, ramener le sang douloureux au bord de tes plaies sèches!

Et cela, nous le pouvons et nous allons le faire, en violant la quiétude de ton Corps, profanateur des amples vices, abstracteur des puretés stupides, Nazaréen maudit, roi fainéant, Dieu lâche!

Vois, grand Satan, ce symbole de la chair de celui qui voulait purger la Terre de plaisir et qui, au nom de la "Justice" chrétienne, a causé la mort de millions de nos frères honorés. Nous plaçons sur toi notre malédiction et nous salissons ton nom.

O Majesté Infernale, condamne-le à l'Abîme, pour qu'il souffre éternellement une angoisse infinie. Frappe-le de ta colère, ô Prince des Ténèbres, et brise-le pour qu'il connaisse l'étendue de ta colère. Appelle tes Légions, pour qu'elles observent ce que nous faisons en Ton Nom. Envoie tes messagers pour proclamer cette action, et fais fuir les sbires chrétiens, titubant vers leur perdition. Frappe-les à nouveau, ô Seigneur de Lumière, pour faire trembler d'horreur ses Anges, ses Chérubins et ses Séraphins, qui se prosterneront devant toi et respecteront ton Pouvoir. Fais que s'écroulent les portes du Paradis, pour venger le meurtre de nos ancêtres!

Thou, thou whom, in my capacity of Priest, I
force, whether thou wilt or no, to descend into
this host, to incarnate thyself into this bread,
Jesus, artisan of hoaxes, bandit of homages,
robber of affection—hear! Since the day when
thou didst issue from the complaisant bowels
of a false virgin, thou hast failed all thy
engagements, belied all thy promises. Centuries have wept awaiting thee, fugitive god,
mute god! Thou wast to redeem man and thou
hast not; thou wast to appear in thy glory, and
thou sleepest. Go, lie, say to the wretch who ap-
peals to thee, "Hope, be patient, suffer; the
hospital of souls will receive thee; angels will succour thee;
Heaven opens to thee." Imposter! Thou knowest
well that the Angels, disgusted at thy inertness,
abandon thee! Thou wast to be the interpreter
of our plaints, the chamberlain of our tears;
thou was to convey them to the cosmos and
thou hast not done so, for this intercession
would disturb thy eternal sleep of happy satiety.

Thou has forgotten the poverty thou didst
preach, vassal enamoured of banquets! Thou
hast seen the weak crushed beneath the press of
profit while standing by and preaching servility!
Oh, the hypocrisy!

That man should accept such woe unto himself is
testimony to his blindness—that very affliction
thou didst credit thyself to cure. O lasting foulness
of Bethlehem, we would have thee confess thy im-
pudent cheats, thy inexpiable crimes! We would

drive deeper the nails into thy hands, press down
the crown of thorns upon thy brow, and bring
blood from the dry wounds of thy sides.

And this we can and *will* do by violating the
quietude of thy body, profaner of the ample
vices, abstractor of stupid purities, cursed
Nazarene, impotent king, fugitive god!
Behold, great Satan, this symbol of the flesh
of him who would purge the Earth of pleasure
and who, in the name of Christian "justice" has
caused the death of millions of our honored
Brothers. We curse him and defile his name.

O Infernal Majesty, condemn him to the Pit,
evermore to suffer in perpetual anguish. Bring
Thy wrath upon him, O Prince of Darkness, and
rend him that he may know the extent of Thy anger.
Call forth Thy legions that they may witness what
we do in Thy name. Send forth thy messengers
to proclaim this deed, and send the Christian
minions staggering to their doom. Smite him
anew, O Lord of Light, that his angels, cherubim,
and seraphim may cower and tremble with fear,
prostrating themselves before Thee in respect
of Thy power. Send crashing down the gates of
Heaven, that the murders of our ancestors
may be avenged!

[The celebrant inserts the wafer into the vagina of the altar,
removes it, holds it aloft to the Baphomet and says:]

CELEBRANT:

Disparais dans le Néant, toi le sot parmi
les sots, toi le vil et détesté, prétendant
à la majesté de Satan! Disparais dans le
Néant du ciel vide, car tu n'as jamais
existé, et tu n'existeras jamais.

Vanish into nothingness, thou fool of fools,
thou vile and abhorred pretender to the
majesty of Satan! Vanish into the void of thy
empty Heaven, for thou wert never, nor
shalt thou ever be.

[The celebrant then raises the wafer and dashes it to the
floor, where it is trampled by himself and the deacon and
subdeacon, while the gong is struck continually. The celebrant then takes the chalice into his hands, faces the altar,
and before drinking recites the following:]

CELEBRANT:

Calicem voluptatis carnis accipiam, et nomen Domini Inferi
invocabo.

[He drinks from the chalice, then turns toward the assembled company, the chalice extended before him. He presents
the chalice with the following words:]

CELEBRANT:

Ecce calix voluptatis carnis, qui laetitiam vitae donat.

[The celebrant then presents the cup to each of the
members of the assemblage, first to the deacon, followed

[by the subdeacon, then the others in order of rank and/or seniority in the Order. In administering the cup to each, he uses the following words:]

CELEBRANT:
Accipe calicem voluptatis carnis in nomine Domini Inferi.

[When all have drunk, the drained chalice is replaced on the altar, the paten placed on top of it, and the veil placed over both. The celebrant then extends his hands, palms downward, and recites the concluding statement:]

CELEBRANT:
Placeat tibi, Domine Satanas, obsequium servitutis meae; et praesta ut sacrificuum quod occulis tuae majestatis indignus obtuli, tibi sit acceptabile, mihique et omnibus pro quibus illud obtuli.

[He then bows before the altar and turns to give the blessing of Satan to the assemblage, extending his left hand in the *Cornu* (Sign of the Horns) and says:]

CELEBRANT:
Ego vos benedictio in nomine Magni Dei Nostri Satanas.

[All assembled company rise, face altar and raise arms in the *Cornu.*]

CELEBRANT:
Ave, Satanas!

All:
Ave, Satanas!

CELEBRANT:
Let us depart; it is done.

DEACON AND SUBDEACON:
So it is done.

[The celebrant, deacon, and subdeacon bow toward the altar, turn and depart. The candles are snuffed and all leave the chamber.]

Epilogue

The Invention, Development, and Prognosis of Christ

1. Year 1 c.e.   An idea
2. Year 100 c.e.   The Son of God

3. Year 1800 c.e.   The acme of human perfection
4. Year 1900 c.e.   A great teacher
5. Year 1950 c.e.   A revolutionary
6. Year 1970 c.e.   A fallible, representative man
7. Year 1975 c.e.   A *symbolic* image, representative of a human type.
8. Year 1985 c.e.   A descriptive word with an interesting origin.
9. Year 2000 c.e.   A well-known folk myth.

L'AIR EPAIS

THE CEREMONY OF THE STIFLING AIR

Along the shore the cloud waves break,
The twin suns sink behind the lake,
The shadows lengthen

                    In Carcosa.

Strange is the night where black stars rise,
And strange moons circle through the skies,
But stranger still is

                    Lost Carcosa.

Songs that the Hyades shall sing,
Where flap the tatters of the King,
Must die unheard in

                    Dim Carcosa.

Song of my soul, my voice is dead,
Die thou, unsung, as tears unshed
Shall dry and die in

                    Lost Carcosa.

—Robert W. Chambers
"Casilda's Song" from *The King in Yellow*

The Ceremony of the Stifling Air is the rite which was performed when entering the sixth degree of the *Order of the Knights Templar*. It celebrates a reawakening of the flesh and a rejection of past self-denials, and symbolic rebirth is attained through a contrived entombment. The ceremony originated in the thirteenth century. In its original form it was not the historical parody into which it later developed. Accounts of the performance of *L'Air Epais* ultimately strengthened the charges of King Philip IV of France in his campaign to abolish the rich order, which was banished in 1331.

The Templars had been exposed to the dualistic concepts of the Yezidis in the Near East. They had seen pride glorified and life praised as never before, when they entered the Courtyard of the Serpent and the Sanctuary of the Peacock, where indulgence became tantamount to greater power. As a result, they developed what was destined to become one of the most significant rites of Satanism. Martyrdom, once believed desirable, was considered with disgust and ridicule, and fierce pride was to become the Templars' last image to the world.

The philosophy of Sheik Adi and the Yezidis, applied to the already acquired wealth and physical resources of the Templars, might have eventually drawn the Western world away from Christianity if not stopped. Even with the banishment of the Templars, their combination of prideful, life-adoring principles joined with Western goal-oriented materialism did not wholly succumb, as borne out by any history of post-Templar fraternal orders.

As the Templars had gained power, they had become more materialistic and less spiritual minded. Rites such as *The Stifling Air*, therefore, presented timely and compatible statements to men who had turned from their earlier heritage of self-sacrifice, abstinence and poverty.

The fraternal attainment conferred by *L'Air Epais* would correspond to the thirty-fourth degree of Freemasonry, if such a grade existed. The present Scottish Rite ends at the Thirty-second degree (Master of the Royal Secret), with an additional degree conferred under honorary circumstances. Correspondingly exalted status is attained in York Rite Masonry at its tenth grade, which carries the title of Knight Templar.

The original Templars' rite of the Fifth degree symbolically guided the candidate through the Devil's Pass in the mountains separating the East from the West (the Yezidi domain). At the fork of the trail the candidate would make an important decision: either to retain his present identity, or strike out on the Left-Hand Path to Schamballah, where he might dwell in Satan's household, having rejected the foibles and hypocrisies of the everyday world.

A striking American parallel to this rite is enacted within the mosques of the *Ancient Arabic Order of the Nobles of the Mystic Shrine*, an order reserved for thirty-second degree Masons. The *Nobles* have gracefully removed themselves from any implication of heresy by referring to the place beyond the Devil's Pass as the domain where they might "worship at the shrine of Islam."

L'Air Epais is impossible to perform without an indiscreet degree of blasphemy toward the Christian ethic, hence its exclusion from Masonic ritual, thereby halting any further progression beyond the Thirty-third degree Scottish Rite and Tenth grade York Rite level. The *Order of the Rosy Cross* of Aleister Crowley's magic curriculum provided an interesting comparison in its Seventh degree (*Adeptus Exemptus*). In that rite, the alternative to taking the Left-Hand Path was to become a Babe of the Abyss, which is not as contradictory and confusing as it sounds, if one considers Crowley's ofttimes Machiavellian modus operandi. Crowley, nobody's fool, simply set up a magical maze so that students whose consciences would only allow them to tread the Right-Hand Path would nevertheless wind up on the Left. Fortunately, precious few of Crowley's disciples progressed as far as the grade of *Adeptus Exemptus*, thus neatly preventing problems that might have arisen from such rude spiritual awakenings.

The overtly anti-Christian sentiments of *The Ceremony of the Stifling Air* classified it as a "Black Mass," according to the accounts that were employed to indict the Templars.

Upon assuming the Sixth degree, a candidate renounced all life-denying spirituality and acknowledged an understanding of the material world as a prerequisite to higher planes of existence. This is a ritual of the death-defiant and allows any unconscious death motivations to be exorcised. It is a statement of rebirth, of the delights of life as opposed to the negation of death. The celebrant in the original version of *L'Air Epais* is represented as a saint, martyr, or other paragon of selflessness. This is done to emphasize the transition from self-denial to self-indulgence.

The ceremony of rebirth takes place in a large coffin. The coffin contains an unclad woman whose task is to awaken lust in the "dead" man who joins her. *L'Air Epais* can serve a twofold purpose; as a rejection of death and a dedication to life, or a blasphemy against those who crave misery, distress, and negation. A celebrant who is basically life loving can release all needs for self-abasement by willingly "dying," thereby exorcising the self-destructive motivations he might be harboring.

L'Air Epais is a ceremony through which one might get the idea of death over with and out of his system, while turning death's accouterments into instruments of lust and life. The coffin, the principle device, contains the manifestation of the force that is stronger than death, the lust that produces new life. This is similar to the coffin symbolism that, with a euphemistic veneer, is found in most lodge rituals.

If the celebrant is patently masochistic, he can, through transference, become a surrogate for members of the congregation who may harbor the same propensity. He suffers a fate worse than death when, within the coffin, instead of experiencing the hoped-for spiritual reward, he is confronted with unexpected passions from which he has long abstained. (If a homophile portrays the celebrant, the coffin should contain another male. In all aspects of the ritual, the element of pleasure should be whatever would most likely be denied in the celebrant's life.) The gravest punishment is always incurred by one whose abstinence has become his indulgence. Thus be warned: to the chronic lover of distress, ruin arrives through the bestowal of indulgence. This, then, can function as a literal interpretation of the phrase, "to kill with kindness."

When a "man of God" is portrayed by the celebrant, as in the later commemorative version of *L'Air Epais*, the ritual will serve to weaken the collective structure of the organization he represents. This factor introduces an element of the *Messe Noir* into the rite, as mentioned by Lewis Spence and other writers.

The title *Stifling Air* refers both to the tension produced by the contrivedly oppressive atmosphere during the early segments of the ceremony, and the closeness within the coffin.

When the performance of *L'Air Epais* was resumed in 1799, it served as a celebration of the successful curse placed upon Philip and Pope Clement V by Jacques de Molay, the last Grand Master of the Templars, who had been condemned to death along with his Knights. The present text employs the actual curse leveled against the King and the Pope by de Molay. Though the dialogue of the Priest of Satan, the King, and the Pope are presented in modern French prose, the statements of de Molay have been retained in their actual stilted delivery.

James Thompson's diabolical litany of the nineteenth century, *The City of Dreadful Night*, has long been employed as the *Denunciation*. It is doubtful that any words could be better suited to the occasion. Portions of the text appear in Raynouard's drama of 1806, *Les Templiers*.

The numerous manifestations of Satanism in Masonic ritual, for instance, the goat, the coffin, the death's-head, etc., can easily be euphemized, but the rejection of certain values demanded by *L'Air Epais* cannot be cloaked in accepted theologies. Once the celebrant has taken this degree, he embarks upon the Left-Hand Path and chooses Hell in place of Heaven. Besides being both ritual and ceremony, *The Stifling Air* is a *memento mori* carried to its highest power.

Requirements for Performance

The chamber must either be black, or mirrored. A mirrored chamber provides greater confrontation for the celebrant, making him hyperconscious of his role. Mirrors also serve to "rob the soul" according to old tradition. An austere chair is provided in which the celebrant sits during the first part of the ritual. The coffin may be of any type, although a traditional hexagonal style is recommended, as this is the type depicted in the actual sigil of the Sixth degree of the Templars and, combined with the skull and crossbones, is retained in Masonic symbology. The coffin must be large enough to accommodate two persons, hence special construction or modification is likely to be necessary.

The usual devices of Satanic ritual are all employed. Additional accouterments include a cat-o'-nine-tails with which to scourge the celebrant, a cruet for the Wine of Bitterness, and a goblet.

The celebrant (Pope) is attired in tattered and decaying vestments. The King is represented as counsel for the celebrant; he wears rags and a miserable crown made out of cardboard. De Molay is dressed in Satanic splendor, with the mantle of the Templars and the symbols of his office. He carries a sword.

The woman in the coffin should be sensually appealing and seductive, the opposite of the wan, pale concept usually associated with death.

For music suitable to this ritual, refer to *Le Messe Noir*, or employ Berlioz' "Funeral and Triumphal Symphony."

Procedure for Performance

The ceremony begins in the customary manner, as described in *The Satanic Bible*. The *Twelfth Enochian Key* is read, and the *Tribunal* begins. After the accusations have been made, and the King allowed to intercede on occasion, judgment is passed and the priest reads the *Denunciation* (*City of Dreadful Night*). Stopping halfway through the *Denunciation*, the priest signals that the Wine of Bitterness be proffered to the celebrant who, accepting his last drink, listens while the litany is completed, after which the priest signals to make ready for the final abasement and joy for the celebrant. The lictors (guards) remove the celebrant from his seat and place him, face downward, on the coffin's lid. The priest then reads Biblical passage, *Hebrews* 1:6–12.

After the scourging, the celebrant is lifted from the lid of the coffin. The priest then knocks three times on the coffin with a staff or the pommel of the sword. A scream is heard from within the coffin, and the lid lifts from inside. The occupant's arms beckon seductively. The celebrant is lowered into the coffin by the lictors, who leave him to his doom or renewal, as the case may be. As the infusion takes place in the coffin, the priest reads the *Thirteenth Enochian Key*. When the infusion is complete, the woman within shouts "*Assez!*" (Enough!), and the celebrant is removed from the coffin and directed by the priest to speak. The celebrant proclaims his homage to Satan, and, showing his new allegiance, casts aside his symbols of martyrdom.

The priest calls for the King, ostensibly to pursue his case. It is discovered that the King has disappeared. He has been banished to the place of eternal indecision and regret, where he must stand in a humorless wind, his tatters blowing, with none to see . . . forever.

The priest presents his final proclamation and the ceremony is closed in the standard manner.

L'AIR EPAIS

The Tribunal

[The priest introduces the participants: his High Court convenes tonight, he says, to hear the case of Pope Clement and the King of France, Philip, who are accused of conspiracy, murder, and treason. He then asks Clement to justify his actions:]

POPE:
Je ne puis comprendre ce mystère.
Un malédiction d'une énorme puissance
est attachée à ma personne et à mes
actes. Les Templiers se sout vengés;
Ils ont de'touit le Pape, ils ont de'touit
le Roi. Leur pouvoir n'est-il pas
arrêté par la mort?

Why am I here? What is the meaning
of this? I cannot comprehend the mystery
of my presence in this place. It is as if a
strange and overpowering summons intrudes
upon my rest. A curse must be upon me
yet, for even after death, the torment of
the Templars is not still. They have destroyed this Pope, and with me they have

taken the King. Yet here am I as it was in
centuries past. Will not their power stop
with death?

KING:
La question est vieille et oubliée.

The matter is old and should be forgotten.

PRIEST:
La question ne peut pas être oubliée.
Beaucoup d'hommes moururent,
parmi les plus braves de France.

The matter cannot be forgotten. Many
men died, among the bravest in France.

POPE:
Ce n'est pas moi qui les ai condamnés.
Leur Roi, Phillipe, connaisait les
actions des Templiers: il obtient des
informatious. Il considère leur for-
tune, leur pouvoir, leur arrogance,
et leurs rites étranges, sombres et
terribles. Il les condamné . . . a mort!

I did not condemn them. The King,
Philip, condemned them when he was in-
formed of their indiscretions. He obtained
damning evidence against the Templars. He

had no choice, when confronted with the evidence. They had wealth beyond their station, and power as well. They had become arrogant in their manner towards the guardians of decency. They conducted strange, dark rites, unholy and terrible, which violated the precincts of the Church. So he condemned them to death. It was only right.

DE MOLAY:

Mais en a-t-il le droit? Quel titre le
lui donne? Mes chevaliers et moi,
quand nous avons juré d'assurer la
victoire à l'étendard sacré, de vouer
notre vie et notre noble exemple a
conquérir, défendre et protéger le
Temple, avons-nous à des rois soumis
notre serment?

What right did he have to condemn men to death for such reasons? What title gave him the privilege? My Knights and I swore to insure victory for our sacred banner—to dedicate our lives to the protection of our Temple— yet with it we submitted our pledge to the King that our power would be his to wield.

PRIEST:

L'autorité de Philippe était celle d'un
profane. Il tenta d'ignorer la force
supérieure, le pouvoir des Magiciens
qui ont en ce jour convoqué notre
Haute Cour.

Philip only had the authority of a profane
ruler, and he tried to ignore the superior
force, the power of the Magicians who today
have called·forth this High Court.

[Philip whispers something to the Pope.]

POPE:
Philippe était leur Roi, il était leur
chef. Mais aussi leur guide, leur
guide spirituel. Les Templiers
furent arrogants, ils se prétendirent
supérieurs à toute loi. Il fallait les
écraser, il fallait qu'ils apprennent la
leçon de l'humilité dans les cachots
de leur Roi.

Philip was their King, he was their ruler.
But he was also their guide, their spiritual
guide. The Templars were arrogant, they
claimed to be above all the laws. They had
to be crushed, they had to discover the lesson
of humility in the jails of their King.

DE MOLAY:
Vous direz donc au Roi qui nous
chargea de fers que loin de résister
nous nous sommes offerts on peut
dans les prisons entraîner l'innocence;
Mais l'homme généréux, armé de sa
constance sous le poids de ses fers
n'est jamais abattu.

You will inform the King, whose shackles
bound us, that we offered ourselves to his
cause, yet he wished to find us unworthy and
deemed us anathema because we had our
Temple, and did not wish to sacrifice our
beliefs—our beliefs which gave us inner
strength. One can drag an innocent man into
a prison cell, but if he is armed with inner
strength and is truly generous, he is not de-
based by the weight of his shackles.

KING:
Cela est vrai, Molay. Votre courage
ne feut pas amoindri par la prison et
la torture. Mais vous avez avoué, vous
avez reconnu vos crimes, et ceux de
votre Ordre.

That may be true, Molay. Though your
courage was not lessened by imprisonment
and torture, you did in fact confess your
heresies, your evil crimes and those of your
Order—your unholy acts.

PRIEST:
Vous les avez torturés! Vous avez
traité ces chevaliers, qui toute leur
vie out combattu pour protéger votre
trône, comme vous auriez traité des
meurtriers ou des voleurs!

You tortured them! You treated the Knights
of the Temple, who, in their strength and all

their lives, fought to protect your throne,
as you would have treated murderers or
thieves!

DE MOLAY (to Philip):
Sire, lorsque me distinguant parmi
tous vos sujets, vous répandiez sur
moi d'honorables bienfaits; De jour où
j'obtenais l'illustre préferénce de nom-
mer de mon nom le fils du Roi de
France, aurais-je pu m'attendre à
l'affront solennel de paraître à vos yeux
comme un vil criminel?

Your Majesty, when distinguishing me among
all your subjects, you showered me with honor.
I refer to the day when I received the illustrious
distinction of bestowing my name on the son of
the King of France. Little could I have expected
the solemn insult of appearing later before you
as a vile criminal.

PRIEST:
de Molay, décrivez à la Cour la mort
des Templiers.

de Molay, please tell the Court how the
Templars died.

DE MOLAY:
Un immense bûcher, dressé pour
leur supplice, s'élève en échafaud,

et chaque chevalier croit mériter
l'honneur d'y monter le premier:
mais le Grand-Maître arrive; Il
monte, il les devance. Son front est
rayonnant de gloire et d'espérance:
"Français, souvenez-vous de nos
derniers accents: nous sommes innocents, nous mourons innocents.
L'arrêt qui nous condamne est un
arrêt injuste. Mais il existe ailleurs
un Tribunal auguste que le faible op-
primé jamais n'implore en vain, et
j'ose t'y citer, ô Pontife Romain!
Encore quarante jours! . . . Je t'y vois
comparaître!"

An immense pyre, prepared for torture,
rises as a scaffold. Each Knight wonders
if he will have the honor of being the first
to climb it. But the Grand Master arrives—
the honor is reserved for him—and he proceeds to climb while his Knights look on.
His face radiates glory and vision of what
will come far beyond that moment. He speaks
to the crowd: "People of France, remember
our last words: we are innocent; we die as
innocents. The verdict that condemns us is
an unjust one, but elsewhere an august Tribunal
exists—one which the oppressed *never* implore
in vain, for its judgments are without piety.
I dare to cite you before that tribunal, O
Pope of Rome! Another forty days shall pass
and then you shall appear before it!"

Chacun en frémissant écoutait le
Grand-Maître. Mais quel étonnement,
quel trouble, quel effroi, quand il dit:
"O Philippe! O mon Maître! O mon
Roi! Je te pardonne en vain, ta vie
est condamnée; Au même tribunal je
t'attends dans l'année." De nombreux
spectateurs, émus et consternés
versent des pleurs sur vous, sur ces
infortunés. De tous côtés s'etend la
terreur, le silence. Il semble que
soudain arrive la vengeance. Les
bourreaux interdits n'osent plus ap-
procher; Ils jettent en tremblant le feu
sur le bûcher, et détournent la tête . . .
Une fumée épaisse entoure l'échafaud,
roule et grossit sans cesse; Tout à
coup le feu brille: à l'aspect du trépas
ces braves chevaliers ne se démentent
pas . . .

Everyone in the crowd was trembling, and
shuddered at the pronouncement of the Grand
Master. But even greater shock and fear
swept o'er the crowd when he continued to
speak: "O Philip, my Master, my King!
Even if I could forgive you, it would be in vain,
for your life is condemned. Before the same
tribunal, I expect you within a year!"
Numerous spectators moved by the Grand
Master's curse are shedding tears for you,
Philip, and terror spreads through the silent
throng. It seems the very semblance of

that future vengeance moves into the crowd!
The executioners are terrified and suddenly
have no power to come close. Tremblingly,
they throw their torches on the pyre, and
quickly turn away. Thick smoke surrounds
the scaffold, growing into billows. Suddenly
flames appear and leap up, yet in the sight
of death, these brave knights do not betray
themselves . . .

PRIEST:
Assez!

Enough!

The Denunciation

PRIEST:
O sad Fraternity, do I unfold
    Your dolorous mysteries shrouded from of yore?
Nay, be assured; no secret can be told
    To any who divined it not before:
None uninitiate by many a presage
Will comprehend the language of the message,
    Although proclaimed aloud of evermore.

And yet a man who raves, however mad,
    Who bares his heart and tells of his own fall,
Reserves some inmost secret good or bad:
    The phantoms have no reticence at all:
The nudity of flesh will blush though tameless,

The extreme nudity of bone grins shameless,
    The unsexed skeleton mocks shroud and pall.

"The vilest thing must be less vile than Thou
    From whom it had its being, God and Lord!
    Creator of all woe and sin! abhorred,
Malignant and implacable! I vow

"That not for all Thy power furled and unfurled,
For all the temples to Thy glory built,
    Would I assume the ignominious guilt
Of having made such men in such a world.

"As if a Being, God or Fiend, could reign,
At once so wicked, foolish, and insane,
As to produce men when He might refrain!

"The world rolls round for ever like a mill:
It grinds out death and life and good and ill;
It has no purpose, heart or mind or will.

"While air of Space and Time's full river flow
The mill must blindly whirl unresting so:
It may be wearing out, but who can know?

"Man might know one thing were his sight less dim
That it whirls not to suit his petty whim,
That it is quite indifferent to him.

"Nay, does it treat him harshly as he saith?
It grinds him some slow years of bitter breath,
Then grinds him back into eternal death."

What men are they who haunt these fatal glooms,
    And fill their living mouths with dust of death,

And make their habitations in the tombs,
    And breathe eternal sighs with mortal breath,
And pierce life's pleasant veil of various error
To reach that void of darkness and old terror
    Wherein expire the lamps of hope and faith?

They have much wisdom yet they are not wise,
    They have much goodness yet they do not well
(The fools we know have their own Paradise,
    The wicked also have their proper Hell);
They have much strength but still their doom is stronger,
Much patience but their time endureth longer,
    Much valor but life mocks it with some spell.

They are most rational and yet insane:
    An outward madness not to be controlled;
A perfect reason in the central brain,
    Which has no power, but sitteth wan and cold,
And sees the madness, and foresees as plainly
The ruin in its path, and trieth vainly
    To cheat itself refusing to behold.

And some are great in rank and wealth and power,
    And some renowned for genius and for worth;
And some are poor and mean, who brood and cower
    And shrink from notice, and accept all dearth
Of body, heart and soul, and leave to others
The boons of life: yet these and those are brothers,
    The saddest and the weariest men on earth.

[Wine of Bitterness is proffered to celebrant.]

The hours are heavy on him and the days;
    The burden of the months he scarce can bear;

73

And often in his secret soul he prays
    To sleep through barren periods unaware,
Arousing at some longed-for date of pleasure;
Which having passed and yielded him small treasure,
    He would outsleep another term of care.

And now at last authentic word I bring,
Witnessed by every dead and living thing;
    Good tidings of great joy for you, for all:
There is no God; no fiend with names divine
Made us and tortures us; if we must pine,
    It is to satiate no Being's gall.

We bow down to the universal laws,
Which never had for man a special clause
    Of cruelty or kindness, love or hate;
If toads and vultures are obscene to sight,
If tigers burn with beauty and with might,
    Is it by favor or by wrath of fate?

All substance lives and struggles evermore
Through countless shapes continually at war,
    By countless interactions interknit:
If one is born a certain day on earth,
All times and forces tended to that birth,
    Not all the world could change or hinder it.
I find no hint throughout the Universe
Of good or ill, of blessing or of curse;
    I find alone Necessity Supreme;
With infinite Mystery, abysmal, dark,
Unlighted even by the faintest spark,
    For us the flitting shadows of a dream.

O Brothers of sad lives! they are so brief;
A few short years must bring us all relief:
    Can we not bear these years of laboring breath?

74

But if you would not this poor life fulfil,
Lo, you are free to end it when you will,
    Without the fear of waking after death.

How the moon triumphs through the endless nights!
    How the stars throb and glitter as they wheel
Their thick processions of supernal lights
    Around the blue vault obdurate as steel!
And men regard with passionate awe and yearning
The mighty marching and the golden burning,
    And think the heavens respond to what they feel.

[Ceremony follows progression described in *Procedure for Performance*.]

[Priest closes ceremony in standard manner.]

DAS TIERDRAMA

Should the subduing talisman, the Cross, break, then will come roaring forth the wild madness of the old champions, that insane Berserker rage, of which the northern poets sing. That talisman is brittle, and the day will come when it will pitifully break. The old stone gods will rise from the long-forgotten ruin and rub the dust of a thousand years from their eyes; and Thor, leaping to life with his giant hammer, will crush the Gothic cathedrals!

—Heinrich Heine, 1834

The Devil holds a unique place in German magical tradition. He, or his personification, always triumphs. No matter how methodically he may be relegated to infamy, he invariably winds up the popular favorite. As the inspirer of werewolves, he drove the Goths and Huns to their victories in Europe; as the final protagonist in the *Nibelungensaga*, he destroyed Valhalla and established his own reign on earth. He became the hero, or at least the roguish and considerate villain, of the miracle plays. Throughout the Christian era he has held his own in German literature and drama better than any other character derived from the Bible.

Dramas in which the Devil appeared in short scenes allowed him increasingly lengthy roles, until in many cases he had taken possession of almost the whole play! He was, to be sure, almost always defeated and driven back to Hell with great tumult and uproar, probably to satisfy the sense of righteousness of the public.

Especially since *Faust*, Satan is no longer considered as the personification of unmitigated evil. In *Faust*, though he still quests for human souls, he pities man—as does Nietzsche's *Zarathustra*—and is depressed that those poor earthborn creatures are so narrow-minded and derive so little pleasure from life. Shaw was to echo these sentiments in *Man and Superman*, in which a very obliging Devil does all he can to see to the comforts of his guests in Hell.

Like Shaw's Satan, the German devil is often seen as the catalyst of enlightened and polite behavior, optimistically deserting the misanthropic role of Mephistopheles in *Faust*. The image that eventually was to serve as the basis of contemporary German Satanic ritual can be seen in Carducci's *Hymn to Satan*, in which Satan is lauded as the spirit of progress, the inspirer of all great movements that contribute to the development of civilization and the advancement of mankind. He is the spirit of revolt that leads to freedom, the embodiment of all heresies that liberate. He wins the undivided admiration of man, and finally supercedes Jehovah as the object of worship.

Of the two German rites included here, the *Tierdrama* is the older. The lessons taught by Aesopian allegory are the first essays to instruct man on the pragmatic importance of applied psychology. Aesopian parable, which was recorded as early as 1500 B.C. in Egypt, was late to appear in a German interpretation. As a result, when Gotthold Lessing produced the parables in the eighteenth century, they were readily assimilated into the heretical philosophy that considers the human animal as decidedly inferior in many respects to his all fours cousins.

The substance of the *Tierdrama* is the admission of one's quadruped heritage. The purpose of the ceremony is for the participants to regress willingly to an animal level, assuming animal attributes of honesty, purity and increased sensory perception. The priest who pronounces the Law maintains the cadence and order needed to remind each participant that though he is an animal, he is still a man. It is this that gives the *Tierdrama* its profound effect.

The rite was originally performed by the *Order of the Illuminati*, founded in 1776 by Adam Weishaupt as an extension of existing Masonic ritual. Ten years earlier, Gotthold Lessing had influenced many Germans' opinions on the limits of the arts with his critical treatise, *Laocoön*. The intellectual climate in Germany had reached the point of controversy that in England gave rise to the *Hell Fire Club*. Passing off the Bavarian *Illuminati* as a society with a purely political base is a blunder often made by those who naively think that politics and magic ritual do not mix. Masonic orders have contained the most influential men in many governments, and virtually every occult order has many Masonic roots.

The rites of the *Illuminati* became the basis of the curriculum of the later *Ordo Templi Orientis*, founded in 1902 by Karl Kellner and Adolf Wilbrandt. A similar curriculum, with strong Rosicrucian overtones, was in the English *Order of the Golden Dawn* in 1887.

The teachings of the *Illuminati* hold that all is material, that all religions are of human invention, that God is man, and man is God, and the world is his kingdom. The *Tierdrama* reinforces this message. It was first performed by Dieter Hertel in Munich, 31 July 1781; the present manuscript dates from 1887.

Many authors have written segments of the *Litany* into literature and drama. It is apparent that a great many writers were members of the Order, or of groups which developed from it. Vivid examples are to be found in the works of Arthur Machen, W. B. Yeats, Robert W. Chambers and James Thompson. Works notable for their reflections of the *Tierdrama* are H. G. Wells's most Satanic work, *The Island of Dr. Moreau*, which employs portions of the *Litany* in a masterful sequence; J. V. Widmann's *Der Heilige und die Tiere*, a bitter diatribe on the animals' behalf against the Christian god; Carl Hauptmann's *Krieg, ein Tedeum*, in which the animals portray the heads of various European powers, and behave no differently than humans in the long run; and of course George Orwell's *Animal Farm* and Aldous Huxley's *Ape and Essence*. It is likely that Aelister Crowley was familiar with the ceremony, as his *Book of the Law* bears a subtle hint in its title to the credo of the *Tierdrama*, the *Litany of the Law*.

The message of Nietzsche's *Zarathustra*, that advises an identification with the beast as a prerequisite to the role of God-man, is eloquently ritualized in the *Tierdrama's* Law of the Jungle. It is a lesson too often neglected by "civilized" man.

Requirements for Performance

Participants consist of a priest who opens the ceremony, three assistants, an altar, an invocator, and participants. The priest acts as master of the ceremony and presides over the entire rite. His assistants are an illuminator to supply light for reading, a gong-striker, and a lictor.

The priest wears a black robe with open hood attached. His assistants wear black robes with closed hoods. The lictor holds a large bullwhip in his right hand, which is gloved in black leather. His left hand is encased in black velvet or satin and there is a ruby on the first finger. A nude female altar sits facing the gathering in the "Bast enthroned" position: upright on a platform against the wall, her legs folded crosswise under her. The invocator and the participants wear black robes with open hoods revealing masks in the likenesses of various animals. Entire animal heads made of papier-maché or other material can heighten the effectiveness. Masks should be as representational as possible, the only exception the invocator, who appears as a lycanthropic half-man, half-beast. He carries a heavy staff which he pounds on the ground when emphasizing portions of the *Litany*.

Robes are mandatory: they represent a formal transition between beast and man.

The ceremony is performed in a chamber with an open area large enough for all of the participants to gather in a semicircle. The priest and his assistants stand to either side of the altar during the *Litany*. This rite can be performed out-of-doors, ideally in a clearing in the woods or some area where the participants can enter through the foliage at the required time. If it is performed outdoors, the woman who serves as the altar should sit on an elevated boulder or log, so that her exalted position will be clearly stated. Torches may be employed outdoors, though it is not required. *Where there is fire hazard to foliage or wildlife the entire purpose of the rite is defeated, so caution is mandatory.*

Incidental music for the *Tierdrama* must be perfectly scored to the *Litany* and action or it will detract from rather than add to the mood. Without a doubt, Richard Strauss's *Also sprach Zarathustra* is most appropriate, if properly cued, and Stravinsky's *Le Sacre du Printemps*. In addition to the gong, a deep-toned drum can be added.

As the ceremony opens, only the priest, his assistants, and the altar are present. A mouse in a cage is placed near the altar, in view of the participants.

DAS TIERDRAMA

[The ceremony is begun according to the standard sequence. The lictor stands in front and to the left of the altar, the gong-striker in front and to the right. The illuminator is behind the priest, who stands inside the diamond, thus formed while he performs the opening rubrics. The *Second Enochian Key* is employed. The chalice is not completely drained. Names are called which have animal counterparts: Bast, Typhon, Fenriz, Midgard, Behemoth, Pan, etc. When the priest concludes the preliminary invocation, he retires to the periphery of the clearing and the invocator enters. After gazing around the clearing, he stands in the center and motions to the illuminator, who steps forward with his light. He is about to summon the beasts. They will enter single file if the rite is performed within a chamber, or if outdoors, through openings in the foliage around the clearing. The gait of each participant should suggest the movements of the beast he represents. The invocator begins the *Litany* and the gong is heard softly, as if calling with the invocator. As he chants, the beasts appear, gradually gathering round him.]

INVOCATOR:
Ich bin der Sprecher des Gesetzes. Hier
sind alle, die neu sind um das Gesetz zu

lernen. Ich stehe im Dunkeln und spreche
das Gesetz. Kein entkommen! Grausam
ist die Strafe für solche, die das Gesetz
brechen. Kein entkommen! Für jeden ist
das Wollen schlecht. Was Du willst, wir
wissen es nicht. Wir werden es wissen!
Manche wollen den Dingen folgen, die sich
bewegen aufpassen, schleichen, warten,
springen um zu töten und zu beissen, beisse
tief und reichlich, sauge das Blut. Manche
wollen mit den Zähnen weinen und die Dinge
mit den Händen aufwühlen und sich in die
Erde hinein kuscheln. Manche klettern auf
die Bäume, manche kratzen an den Gräben
des Todes, manche kampfen mit der Stirn,
den Füssen oder Klauen, manche beissen
plätzlich zu ohne Veranlassung! Die
Bestraffung ist streng und gewiss. Deswegen
lerne das Gesetz. Sage die Wörter! . . . Sage
die Wörter! Sage die Wörter!

I am the Sayer of the Law. Here come all
that be new, to learn the Law. I stand in
the darkness and say the Law. None escape!
Cruel are the punishments of those who
break the Law. None escape! For every
one the want is bad, what *you* want of us,
we know not, yet we shall know. Some
want to follow things that move, to watch
and slink and wait and spring, to kill and
bite, bite deep and rich, sucking the blood!
Some want to tear with teeth and hands into
the roots of things, snuffing into the earth!
Some go clawing trees; some go scratching
at the graves of the dead; some go fighting

with foreheads or feet or claws; some bite
suddenly without giving warning. Punishment is sharp and sure, therefore learn
the Law. Say the words! Learn the Law.
Say the words! Say the words!

INVOCATOR:
Nicht auf allen Vieren zu gehen: das ist das
Gesetz. Sind wir nicht Menschen?

Not to go on all fours: that is the Law. Are
we not men?

BEASTS:
Nicht auf allen Vieren zu gehen: das ist das
Gesetz. Sind wir nicht Menschen?

Not to go on all fours: that is the Law. Are
we not men?

INVOCATOR:
Nicht die Rinde oder Bäume zu zerkratzen:
das ist das Gesetz. Sind wir nicht Menschen?

Not to claw bark or trees:
that is the Law. Are we not men?

BEASTS:
Nicht die Rinde oder Bäume zu zerkratzen:
das ist das Gesetz. Sind wir nicht Menschen?

Not to claw bark or trees: that is the Law.
Are we not men?

INVOCATOR:

Nicht zu murren und zu brüllen: das ist das
Gesetz. Sind wir nicht Menschen?

Not to snarl or roar: that is the Law.
Are we not men?

BEASTS:

Nicht zu murren und zu brüllen: das ist das
Gesetz. Sind wir nicht Menschen?

Not to snarl or roar: that is the Law.
Are we not men?

INVOCATOR:

Nicht unsere Fangzähne im Zorn zu zeigen:
das ist das Gesetz. Sind wir nicht Menschen?

Not to show our fangs in anger: that is the
Law. Are we not men?

BEASTS:

Nicht unsere Fangzähne im Zorn zu zeigen:
das ist das Gesetz. Sind wir nicht Menschen?

Not to show our fangs in anger: that is the
Law. Are we not men?

INVOCATOR:

Nicht unsere Zugehörigkeit zu zerstoren:
das ist das Gesetz. Sind wir nicht Menschen?

Not to destroy our belongings: that is the
Law. Are we not men?

BEASTS:
Nicht unsere Zugehörigkeit zu zerstoren:
das ist das Gesetz. Sind wir nicht Menschen?

Not to destroy our belongings: that is the
Law. Are we not men?

INVOCATOR:
Nicht zu töten ohne zu denken: das ist das
Gesetz. Sind wir nicht Menschen?

Not to kill without thinking: that is the Law.
Are we not men?

BEASTS:
Nicht zu töten ohne zu denken: das ist das
Gesetz. Sind wir nicht Menschen?

Not to kill without thinking: that is the Law.
Are we not men?

INVOCATOR:
Der Mensch ist Gott.

Man is God.

BEASTS:
Der Mensch ist Gott.

Man is God.

INVOCATOR:
Wir sind Menschen.

We are men.

BEASTS:
Wir sind Menschen.

We are men.

INVOCATOR:
Wir sind Götter.

We are Gods.

BEASTS:
Wir sind Götter.

We are Gods.

INVOCATOR:
Gott ist der Mensch.

God is Man.

BEASTS:
Gott ist der Mensch.

God is Man.

INVOCATOR:
Sein ist das Haus des Schmerzes.

His is the house of pain.

BEASTS:
Sein ist das Haus des Schmerzes.

His is the house of pain.

INVOCATOR:
Sein ist die Hand die Schafft.

His is the hand that makes.

BEASTS:
Sein ist die Hand die Schafft.

His is the hand that makes.

INVOCATOR:
Sein ist die Hand die verletzt.

His is the hand that wounds.

BEASTS:
Sein ist die Hand die verletzt.

His is the hand that wounds.

INVOCATOR:
Sein ist die Hand die heilt.

His is the hand that heals.

BEASTS:
Sein ist die Hand die heilt.

His is the hand that heals.

INVOCATOR:
Sein ist der leuchtende Blitz.

His is the lightning flash.

BEASTS:
Sein ist der leuchtende Blitz.

His is the lightning flash.

INVOCATOR:
Sein ist die tiefe See.

His is the deep salt sea.

BEASTS:
Sein ist die tiefe See.

His is the deep salt sea.

INVOCATOR:
Sein sind die Sterne und der Himmel.

His are the stars in the sky.

BEASTS:
Sein sind die Sterne und der Himmel.

His are the stars in the sky.

INVOCATOR:
Sein sind die Gesetze des Landes.

His are the rulers of the land.

BEASTS:
Sein sind die Gesetze des Landes.

His are the rulers of the land.

INVOCATOR:
Sein ist der Ort genannt Himmel.

His is the place called Heaven.

BEASTS:
Sein ist der Ort genannt Himmel.

His is the place called Heaven.

INVOCATOR:
Sein ist der Ort genannt Hölle.

His is the place called Hell!

BEASTS:
Sein ist der Ort genannt Hölle.

His is the place called Hell!

INVOCATOR:
Sein ist was ist unseres.

His is what is ours!

BEASTS:
Sein ist was ist unseres.

His is what is ours!

INVOCATOR:
Er ist was wir sind.

He is what we are!

BEASTS:
Er ist was wir sind.

He is what we are!

INVOCATOR:
Ich bin der Sprecher des Gesetzes. Hier
sind alle, die neu sind um das Gesetz zu
lernen. Ich stehe im Dunkeln und spreche
das Gesetz. Kein entkommen!

I am the Sayer of the Law. Here come all
that be new, to learn the Law. I stand in
the darkness and say the Law. None escape!

BEASTS:
Kein entkommen!

None escape!

INVOCATOR:
Grausam ist die Strafe für solche, die das
Gesetz brechen. Kein entkommen!

Cruel are the punishments of those who
break the Law. None escape!

BEASTS:
Kein entkommen!

None escape!

INVOCATOR:

Für jeden ist das Wollen schlecht. Was Du
willst, wir wissen es nicht. Wir werden
es wissen!

For every one the want is bad, what you
want of us, we know not, yet we shall know.

BEASTS:

Wir werden es wissen!

We shall know!

INVOCATOR:

Manche wollen den Dingen folgen, die sich
bewegen aufpassen, schleichen, warten,
sprigen um zu töten und zu beissen, beisse
tief und reichlich, sauge das Blut. Manche
wollen mit den Zähnen winen und die Dinge
mit den Händen aufwühlen und sich in die Erde
hinein kuscheln. Manche klettern auf die
Bäume, manche kratzen an den Gräben des
Todes, manche kämpfen mit der Stirn, den
Füssen oder Klauen, manche beissen plätzlich
zu ohne Veranlassung! Die Bestraffung ist
streng und gewiss. Deswegen lerne das
Gesetz. Sage die Wörter! . . . Sage die
Wörter! Sage die Wörter!

Some want to follow things that move, to
watch and slink and wait and spring, to kill
and bite, bite deep and rich, sucking the

94

blood! Some want to tear with teeth and hands into the roots of things, snuffing into the earth! Some go clawing trees, some go scratching at the graves of the dead; some go fighting with foreheads or feet or claws; some bite suddenly without giving warning. Punishment is sharp and sure, therefore learn the Law. Say the words! Learn the Law. Say the words! Say the words!

INVOCATOR:
Nicht auf allen Vieren zu gehen: das ist das Gesetz. Sind wir nicht Menschen?

Not to go on all fours: that is the Law. Are we not men?

BEASTS:
Nicht auf allen Vieren zu gehen: das ist das Gesetz. Sind wir nicht Menschen?

Not to go on all fours: that is the Law. Are we not men?

INVOCATOR:
Nicht die Rinde oder Bäume zu zerkratzen: das ist das Gesetz. Sind wir nicht Menschen?

Not to claw bark or trees: that is the Law. Are we not men?

BEASTS:
Nicht die Rinde oder Bäume zu zerkratzen: das ist das Gesetz. Sind wir nicht Menschen?

Not to claw bark or trees: that is the Law.
Are we not men?

INVOCATOR:
Nicht zu murren und zu brüllen: das ist das
Gesetz. Sind wir nicht Menschen?

Not to snarl or roar: that is the Law.
Are we not men?

BEASTS:
Nicht zu murren und zu brüllen: das ist das
Gesetz. Sind wir nicht Menschen?

Not to snarl or roar: that is the Law.
Are we not men?

INVOCATOR:
Nicht unsere Fangzähne im Zorn zu zeigen:
das ist das Gesetz. Sind wir nicht Menschen?

Not to show our fangs in anger: that is the
Law. Are we not men?

BEASTS:
Nicht unsere Fangzähne im Zorn zu zeigen:
das ist das Gesetz. Sind wir nicht Menschen?

Not to show our fangs in anger: that is the
Law. Are we not men?

INVOCATOR:
Nicht unsere Zugehörigkeit zu zerstoren:

das ist das Gesetz. Sind wir nicht Menschen?

Not to destroy our belongings: that is the
Law. Are we not men?

BEASTS:
Nicht unsere Zugehörigkeit zu zerstoren:
das ist das Gesetz. Sind wir nicht Menschen?

Not to destroy our belongings: that is the
Law. Are we not men?

INVOCATOR:
Nicht zu töten ohne zu denken: das ist das
Gesetz. Sind wir nicht Menschen?

Not to kill without thinking: that is the Law.
Are we not men?

BEASTS:
Nicht zu töten ohne zu denken: das ist das
Gesetz. Sind wir nicht Menschen?

Not to kill without thinking: that is the Law.
Are we not men?

INVOCATOR:
Der Mensch ist Gott.

Man is God.

BEASTS:
Der Mensch ist Gott.

Man is God.

INVOCATOR:
Wir sind Menschen.

We are men.

BEASTS:
Wir sind Menschen.

We are men.

INVOCATOR:
Wir sind Götter.

We are Gods.

BEASTS:
Wir sind Götter.

We are Gods.

INVOCATOR:
Gott ist der Mensch.

God is Man.

BEASTS:
Gott ist der Mensch.

God is Man.

INVOCATOR:
Sein ist das Haus des Schmerzes.

His is the house of pain.

BEASTS:
Sein ist das Haus des Schmerzes.

His is the house of pain.

INVOCATOR:
Sein ist die Hand die schafft.

His is the hand that makes.

BEASTS:
Sein ist die Hand die schafft.

His is the hand that makes.

INVOCATOR:
Sein ist die Hand die verletzt.

His is the hand that wounds.

BEASTS:
Sein ist die Hand die verletzt.

His is the hand that wounds.

INVOCATOR:
Sein ist die Hand die heilt.

His is the hand that heals.

BEASTS:
Sein ist die Hand die heilt.

His is the hand that heals.

INVOCATOR:
Sein ist der leuchtende Blitz.

His is the lightning flash.

BEASTS:
Sein ist der leuchtende Blitz.

His is the lightning flash.

INVOCATOR:
Sein ist die tiefe See.

His is the deep salt sea.

BEASTS:
Sein ist die tiefe See.

His is the deep salt sea.

INVOCATOR:
Sein sind die Sterne und der Himmel.

His are the stars in the sky.

BEASTS:
Sein sind die Sterne und der Himmel.

His are the stars in the sky.

INVOCATOR:
Sein sind die Gesetze des Landes.

His are the rulers of the land.

BEASTS:
Sein sind die Gesetze des Landes.

His are the rulers of the land.

INVOCATOR:
Sein ist der Ort genannt Himmel.

His is the place called Heaven.

BEASTS:
Sein ist der Ort genannt Himmel.

His is the place called Heaven.

INVOCATOR:
Sein ist der Ort genannt Hölle.

His is the place called Hell.

BEASTS:
Sein ist der Ort genannt Hölle.

His is the place called Hell.

INVOCATOR:
Sein ist was ist unseres.

His is what is ours.

BEASTS:
Sein ist was ist unseres.

His is what is ours.

INVOCATOR:
Er ist was wir sind.

He is what we are.

BEASTS:
Er ist was wir sind.

He is what we are.

[The invocator drops his staff and slouches forward to the altar, gazing at it with admiration and longing, but proudly exhibiting control and decorum. As he stands, the priest comes forward with the chalice, proffering it to the invocator, who accepts it, raising it in homage to the altar. The invocator drains the chalice noisily but with great solemnity. The priest relieves him of the chalice. The invocator steps forward, raises his arms in a yearning manner, and tenderly strokes the altar's flesh. He steps back and, in reverie, is presented with the sword by the priest. As the beast (invocator) accepts the sword, he studies its symmetry and gleaming length, then grasping it in both paws, raises it on high. The other beasts lift their arms, some attempting to make the *Cornu*—the Sign of the Horns.]

INVOCATOR:
Der Mensch ist Gott.

Man is God.

BEASTS:
Der Mensch ist Gott.

Man is God.

INVOCATOR:
Wir sind Menschen.

We are Men.

BEASTS:
Wir sind Menschen.

We are Men.

INVOCATOR:
Wir sind Götter.

We are Gods.

BEASTS:
Wir sind Götter.

We are Gods.

INVOCATOR:
Gott ist der Mensch.

God is Man.

BEASTS:
Gott ist der Mensch.

God is Man.

INVOCATOR:
HEIL, SATAN!

HAIL, SATAN!

ALL:

HEIL, SATAN!

HAIL, SATAN!

[The invocator lowers the sword and the priest takes it from him. The invocator goes to the caged mouse and releases it.]

INVOCATOR:
Meine Ezählung ist zu Ende. Dort läuft
eine Maus; wir immer sie fängt, mag
sicheine riesige Mütze aus ihrem Pelz
machen.

My tale is done. There runs a mouse:
whoever catches her may make a great,
great cap out of her fur.

[As the mouse runs off, the beasts start to drop on all fours, then restrain themselves and solemnly shuffle out of the clearing, the invocator being last to leave. When all is quiet, the priest moves to the altar and closes the rite in the standard manner.]

THE LAW OF THE TRAPEZOID
DIE ELEKTRISCHEN VORSPIELE

Sturm, Sturm, Sturm, Sturm, Sturm, Sturm!
Läutet die Glocken von Turm zu Turm!
Läutet, dass Funken zu sprühen beginnen . . .
—Dietrich Eckart

If the *Tierdrama*'s theme could be found in much of the
literature and theatre drama of the nineteenth century, *Die
elektrischen Vorspiele*'s theme could be seen in the science-
fantasy cinema of the early twentieth century.

The principle of utilizing electrical and magnetic energy
to effect magical ends is sorely neglected by most occult scholars,
yet is employed with almost maniacal gusto by the contemporary
German school of Satanic magic. As practical applications of
electrical energy increased at the turn of the nineteenth century,
so did opportunities for neo-promethean innovation in the field
of ritual magic.

The German societies *Vril, Thule, Freunden von Lucifer,
Germania*, and *Ahnenerbe*, while maintaining the basic magic
repertoire of the earlier *Illuminati*, became what has been loosely
defined as the *Schwartze Orden*—the *Black Order*—which
flourished during the period between the two World Wars.
Paradoxically, though Freemasonry became anathema during the
Nazi regime, virtually every rite of the *Black Order* employed
Masonic principles.

In addition to some rites of the German *Ordo Templi*

Orientis which utilized sexual energy as a means of magical transmission, the *Black Order* rites also used concepts of geometry, utilized reflective planes, paradoxical sound frequencies, and atmospheric ionization. Ritual chambers looked like sets from the *Schauerfilmen* of the period, and indeed they should have, for they were often designed by the same architects. Angles of non-Euclidian incidence and Lovecraftian aspect were prime visual ingredients.

Ceremonies like *Das Wahsinn der Logisch* (The Madness of Logic) were *Marat/Sade* type playlets in which the craziest patients became the asylum heads, using their standards of behavior as criteria in selecting those they deemed mad enough to be safely released into society. The lunatic became a magic influence on those outside the asylum, and controlled people's actions from the safety of confinement. The principles were employed for real-life ends by real-life Caligaris and Mabuses . . . and still are.

Flashing lights producing stroboscopic effects, electrostatic generators, electric organs with controllable harmonics, scanners, and a mental discipline and emotional response that can temporarily leave its Alpha waves outside the chamber and strive towards Gamma, the ultimate goal: these are the ingredients required for the creation of the is-to-be, as defined in the ritual of the *Electrical Prelude—Die elektrischen Vorspiele.*

Many of the rite's principles relate to the experiments of Wilhelm Reich, a name to be reckoned with in the magic of the future. The procedure is to "charge" the chamber in a manner that allows the celebrant to "draw" energy from it while at the same time he adds his own strength of will. The celebrant's intensity of purpose is further stimulated by the related litany. Upon "peaking," the celebrant enters the reflective planes that will multiply and send forth his will. He remains within the enclosure until he *and the chamber itself* is devoid of all energy, and a negative ionization and deozonization (or in Reichian terminology, DOR) ensues.

The ritual may be attended by several persons: however, the essential working is confined to a single celebrant, who acts as the catalyst. Although additional persons can benefit from participation, the celebrant *can* effectively perform alone. It should be stressed that groups performing *Die elektrischen Vorspiele* did so with a single purpose, and the presence of several persons therefore added to the effectiveness. The rite, as presented here, was intended to alter an existing social climate and establish far-reaching change.

The rite is best performed in a relatively small enclosure, as a large chamber necessitates excessively heavy amounts of electrical discharge in order to attain sufficient ionization. Essentially, the chamber acts as an electrical vacuum tube, with the participants *inside* it serving as oscillators. A Van de Graaff generator, Tesla coil, or other electrostatic generator, with enough power to influence the atmosphere within the chamber, is needed. The device must be exposed, not contained within its own enclosure, hence extreme care must be exercised that bodily contact is not made with the device. It is best placed in an area of the chamber that is inaccessible to persons present to avoid the danger of serious injury or electrocution.

The electrostatic generator should produce electrical discharge which is readily visible, a lightning display that is controlled by the celebrant during the first part of the ritual. In this way he is "dressing" the chamber according to his own emotional responses. There is no arbitrary span of time for this segment, as the duration of the preliminary charging period is dependent upon the size of the enclosure, the extent of electrical discharge, and the human response factor. The lightning is controlled from a console or control panel so placed that there can be a change of operators. The celebrant must be able to leave his station, with an assistant to continue at the console, or make beforehand arrangements for an automated progression. New developments in audio-actuated controls make this a relatively simple procedure.

Lighting is supplied by argon and neon gas filled tubes with the transformers shielded to prevent extraneous sound frequencies. Sound is supplied by some instrument on which not only pitch and intensity may be controlled, but individual harmonics, as well, while producing an expanding (sine) wave for the basic tonal pattern. The now-extinct Compton Electrone and Schilder Klavilux were admirably suited, as are larger model Hammond organs and the Moog Synthesizer. Sounds must fluctuate between 60 cps and 11,000 cps—preferably "pure" tones, although "resultants" are permissible. Beneath and above these frequencies should prevail a continuous emission of "black" and "white" sound, lasting through the entire rite.

The chamber should be designed with what might best be described as "expressionistic" decor, so that all visual images may add to the out-thrusting quality of the ritual. An altar platform at one end of the chamber should be utilized for all necessary artifacts. The unclad woman who customarily serves as a living altar is not required in *Die elektrischen Vorspiele*. In her place, a human skull (*totenkopf*) rests upon a scarlet cushion. In this ritual as in all other satanic rites, the skull serves as a reminder of the material, flesh-and-bone godhead that is man, rather than as a symbol of mortality. It also represents the vault of wisdom from whence all human ideas and developments emerge, the temple of invention, both material and "spiritual." A candlestick bearing a black candle is placed at each side of the skull. The chalice rests directly in front of the skull, with the bell and phallus to either side. The sword rests parallel to the front edge of the platform. The wall above the altar displays the Sigil of Satan.

A pentagonal enclosure, the inside of which is mirrored, serves to receive the celebrant. The pentagon must be large enough in diameter and with walls high enough to receive the celebrant's prone body, yet easy to enter and leave. To be practical, the walls of the pentagon should be no higher than two feet above the surface of the floor, or if sunken, the floor of the pentagon should be no more than that depth beneath the normal floor level. The top edge of the pentagon carries the neon tubing mentioned previously, to mark its boundaries and illuminate its occupant.

Directly above the pentagon hangs an open, regular trapezoid, suspended by strong but lightweight cord, so that the slightest force sets it in motion. The hanging trapezoid, constructed of lightweight material, is wound like an induction coil and can be charged just before the ritual begins. The length of the base of the trapezoid is equal to the length of each segment of the pentagon.

A stroboscopic light is used to illuminate the celebrant within the pentagon, and the frequency of flash should be whatever is most conducive to the celebrant's needed response. In the past, an arc light with a revolving shutter was used, augmented by a continuous image of flames, projected through the principle of the Lobsterscope. However, now there are vastly improved electronic flash units insofar as controlled frequencies are concerned.

Participants wear black ceremonial robes and hoods. The celebrant is bareheaded.

When *Die elektrischen Vorspiele* was performed in Nazi Germany (circa 1932–35) by the intellectual element of the budding *Sicherheitsdienst RFSS*, the banners and symbols of the time were used as an integral part of the decor. Participants were garbed in full dress, whether uniformed or not. Topical music was added—usually *Morgenrot* at the beginning and *Unsre Fahne Flattert uns Voran* as a closing anthem. These were played by the organist or on a gramophone. Music by Richard Wagner may be used instead at the opening and closing of the ritual.

The litany spoken by the celebrant paraphrases the *Eighth*

Emerald Tablet of Thoth (Hermes Trismegistus), in which the Einsteinian time/space continuum is advanced through arcane Greek and Egyptian verbiage.

The windows to the fourth dimension are mirrored planes which multiply the image of the single being. Small wonder that the looking glass has had the reputation as a tool of Lucifer, for beyond its use as the most obvious plaything of pride, it is a tool to find light where none is thought to exist.

The principles of this rite have been recorded in many ways— all similar, yet with nuances unique to each particular order. Versions of the litany in print have catered to the standards of theologically acceptable prose, avoiding what might be offensive to the metaphysically minded. So far as this author has been able to discover, German lodges have kept secret the rites which accompany the spoken hypothesis. It is known that certain individuals have stumbled upon these procedures, employing and expanding upon them to great advantage, but, as might be expected, little has been divulged. The instructions given here will serve as a useful key to those who can extract the most viable principles and apply them to their own ends.

DIE ELEKTRISCHEN
VORSPIELE

Procedure for Performance

Inasmuch as the litany is recited without interruption after the celebrant enters the pentagon, the working procedure is guided almost entirely by rubrics.

1- The ritual begins in the standard manner, with the purification, opening invocation, calling of suitable Infernal Names, partaking of the chalice, invocation of the Four Elements, benediction with phallus, and calling of the *Sixth Enochian Key.*

2- Celebrant takes his place at the console, turns on both black and white sound signals which continue until end of ritual.

3- Begin alternating audible sound at one second intervals (60/11,000 cps).

4- Celebrant activates electrostatic generator until sufficient ozonization and ionization occurs and atmosphere is fully charged.

5- Celebrant activates neon tubing, leaves console.

6- Assistant takes his place at the console, and maintains audible sound at one minute intervals during the celebrant's invocation.

7- Celebrant steps into pentagon and delivers invocation, turning counter clockwise very slowly as he speaks. When he completes his invocation, an assistant relieves him of his text and presents the ceremonial sword or dagger. As the celebrant takes the sword in hand, the assistant at the console reactivates the electrostatic generator, combines both audible frequencies in chording, bringing the volume to full intensity, and activates the stroboscopic illumination.

8- Celebrant holds sword on high, turning slowly counter clockwise, pausing at each reflective plane, until nine planes have been confronted.

9- Celebrant lowers himself into pentagon, sword in hand, and assumes the *hakenkreuz* position while lying on left side, sword in right hand. At that moment the electrostatic generator is turned off, but sound is maintained at full intensity and lights are left flashing. Celebrant remains prostrate within the pentagon until his vision has been cast.

10- Celebrant rises to his feet inside pentagon. Assistant at console turns off strobelight, stops 11,000 cps note completely while maintaining heavy intensity on a sound of combined 30/45/60 cps frequencies, approximating thunder. Celebrant faces east, lifts sword, and begins the Proclamation, to which the congregants respond, arms upraised in the Sign of the Horns.

11- All lower arms and celebrant or assistant closes ritual in the usual manner, with all console controls off, leaving only candlelight, and closing musical anthem played during pollu-tionary.

Die elektrischen Vorspiele

CELEBRANT:
Die Feuer der Hölle sind gegeben und
die Gedanken gewinnen die Oberhand.
Offnet die Portale zur Dunkelheit. Oh
grosser Wegbereiter. Erscheine in diesem
Kreis. Wehe durch die Tore des glänzenden
Trapezohedron für das Blut, welches darge-
boten wurde!

The fire of Hell doth provide and the
thoughts from within doth prevail. Open
the portals of darkness, O Great Opener
of the Way. Come forth into this cycle.
Blast ye forth through the gates of the
shining Trapezohedron, for the blood hath
been offered!

Erscheine unter den Menschen und sei nicht
länger zurückgedrangt. Komm, wehe und
krieche ein in die grossen Konzile ohne
Dich und beende den Weg derer, die uns
aufhalten. Ich sage der Glanz muss gesteigert
werden, offenbare das Gesicht der Schlange.
Bei dem Klang werden wir das Gesicht der

Schlange sehen, so—lerne die Wörter gut,
die nur ein Mensch verkünden kann. Seht,
ich habe den Schleier der Schlange und sende
ihn unter die Menschen. Oh höre! Die
Schlange lebt, an einem Platz, der offen
ist für die Welt.

Appear among men and be driven back no
longer. Come forth and creep into the
great councils of those without, and stop
the way of those who would detain us. I
decree that the glamour be lifted, revealing
the face of the Serpent. By the sounds ye
shall see the face of the Serpent, so learn
well the word that only a man can pronounce.
Thus, I lift the veil from the Serpent and cast
him forth among men. Oh hear! The Serpent
liveth, in a place that is open at times to
the world.

Unsichtbar geht sie mitten unter uns und
so beschleichen wir die Nacht unsichtbar
so gut wie möglich und neu durch die Winkel
mögen wir sichtbar sein und für jene, die
Nicht sehen, seien die Augen geblendet
durch die Mühlsteine der Gerechtigkeit.
Ich sage zu denen, die mit unverständlicher
Zunge reden: Ich weiss sehr wohe, *was*
Euch zurückhält diesen Kreis und verlassen.
Die flüchtigen Jagdhunde der Grenze warten
geduckt auf die Seelen der Gerechtigkeit.
Sie sind die Wächter des Kreises und sie
liegen versteckt auf der Schwelle zur Zeit
und ihre Zeitraumpläne bewegen sich über

ihren, sie verstecken sie gut. Sie bewegen
sich neu durch die Winkel, obgleich sie frei
sind von gekrümmten Abmessungen. Fremd
und entsetzlich sind die Jagdhunde der
Grenze, sie folgen im Bewusstsein der
Begrenzung zum Zeitraum. Unsichtbar
gehen sie mitten unter uns, an jenen Orten,
wo der Ritus gesprochen wurde.

Unseen they walk amongst us, and as we doth
join them, so we stalk the night unseen as well,
for only through the angles can we be seen,
and those without see not, for their eyes are
blinded by millstones of righteousness. I
say unto thee who speaketh with garbled tongue:
I know well *that* which holds ye from leaving
this cycle. I have glimpsed the Hounds of
the Barrier, lying in wait for the souls of the
righteous. They are the guardians of the
cycles, and they lurk at the threshold of time,
and their space-planes move about them,
hiding them well. They move only through
angles, though free are they not of the curved
dimensions. Strange and terrible are the
Hounds of the Barrier, follow they consciousness to the limits of space. Unseen they walk
among thee, in places where the Rites have
been said.

Manche nehmen die Gestalt der Menschen
an, nicht wissend was sie tun und wenn Blut
vergossen wurde, ziehen sie sich nochmals
zurück in die Grotte des Satans, nehmen
die Form an die ich gut kenne. Manche

scheinen zu warten und breiten ihre grossen
Flügel, wissen ganz sicher, dass ich sie
nochmals hervorrufe!

Some take the semblance of men, knowing
not what they do, and when the blood hath been
spilled, retreat they once more into the grotto
of Satan, taking the forms I know well. Some
seeth as they wait, and preen their great
wings, knowing full well that once again I
shall call them forth!

Und die Finsteren der Nacht werden sich
ducken unter ihren Klauen, die mächtigen
Jagdhunde liegen und warten darauf zur
Welt zurückzukehren. Glaube nicht
Mensch mit verdorbenen Gehirn, dass Du
der grossen Bestie entkommen kannst
durch Beschreiten Deines Altar's, sie
folgen schnell durch alle Winkel und sie
sind im Innern des Trapezoid. Ich kenne
sie, da ich einer der ihren bin und die
grosse Schranke erreicht habe und die
zeitlosen Ufer gesehn, sowie die mono-
politischen Gestalten der Grenz jagdhunde.

And the night-gaunts shall ride, and, crouch-
ing at their talons, the great hounds lie a-
waiting to leap forth into the world. Think
not, o men of mildewed minds, that ye can
escape the great beasts by entering thy
shrines, for they follow fast through angles,

and they lurk within the Trapezoid. I know
them for I am as one with them, and I have
approached the great Barrier, and seen on
the shores where time exists not the mono-
lithic forms of the Hounds of the Barrier.

Ha! Ich fand sie versteckt in den Abgrunden
der Zeit weit voraus, sie witterten mich
von Weitem, erhöhten sich, gaben den
grossen durchdringenden Schrei von sich,
der von Kreis zu Kreis gehört wird.
Verweile ich denn im Lager des wilden
Tieres, entfernt vom Menschen, an den
grauen Ufern der Zeit, jenseits des
Weltrandes, wenn sie sich mit mir bewegten,
durch Winkel die niemand kennt. Sie
ducken sich an der dunkeln Schwelle, ihre
Rachen sind heisshunggrig und gefrassig
nach den Seelen derer, die keine haben!

Yea! Hiding in the abyss beyond time I
found them, and they, scenting me afar off,
raised themselves and gave the great bell
cry that can be heard from cycle to cycle.
Dwelt I then, in lairs remote from man,
on the gray shores of time, beyond the world's
rim, and ever with me they moved, in angles
not known to man. On that dark threshold
they crouch, their jaws agape and ravening
for the souls of those who are without!

Ich komme zurück durch die Winkel und
eisern folgten sie mir. Ha! Die Ver-

schlinger folgten und somit wurde ich
der Marschall der Wirte der Hölle, jene
welche mir folgten und sie Hunde führten,
ritten durch den Wirbelwind der Nacht, um
die Erde zu reinigen und das Eis zum
Schmelzen zu bringen!

Returned I through angles back, and hard by
me they followed. Yea! The devourers
followed and thus I was and have become
the marshal of the hosts of Hell, and
those who follow me and walk the Hounds
and ride the whirlwinds of the night, become
an army out from Hell to scourge the earth
and melt the ice!

Durch das Innere der Prismer-Arbeit und
der Dämmerung der Grotte spreche ich
durch die Winkel gespiegelt durch Sinn
und Höhergestelltes. Oh, lerne das Gesetz,
mein Bruder der Nacht—das Grosse Gesetz
und das Niedrige Gesetz. Das Grosse Gesetz
bringt das Gleichgewicht, ist beharrlich ohne
Barmherzigkeit. Das Niedrige Gesetz
verbleibt als Schlussel und der schimmernde
Trapezoid ist die Tür!

From prisms wrought within the twilit grotto
I speak through angles mirrored with thoughts
senescent and supreme. O learn the Law,
my brothers of the night—the Great Law

and the Lesser Law. The Great Law brings
the balance and doth persist without mercy.
The Lesser Law abideth as the key, and the
shining Trapezoid is the door!

O mein Bruder, studiere gut den Stein des
Fluges, unerkannt für jene ohne ihn, innen
warten die grell schimmernden Antlitze
der Jagdhunde die Welt zu entflammen!
Sind die Winkel klein und ruhig oder gigan-
tisch in ihrer brüllenden Gewalttätigkeit,
es ist in der Weise, die wir so gut kennen.
An dieser grimmigen, grauen Küste
herscht der Obelisk und fässt su mit seinen
vier Klauen nach dem Ring des Fafnir-
Führer, diese Verkörperung kommt,
welche uns vergrössert und schlägt jene,
die gegen uns sind.

O my brothers, study well the stone with
planes unrecognized by those without, for
within those glaring facets the Hounds await
that set the world aflame! Be the angles
small and still or gargantuan in their roaring
outrage, the form is that which we know so
well. On the grim, gray shore, the mono-
lith prevails, and clutched within the four-
fold talons of the ring which Fafnir guards,
that shape remains to bring forth that which
gives us increase and smites those who
would oppose us.

Oh, schwaches Mensch, höre meine

123

Warnung, versuche nicht gewaltsam
das Tor zur Zukunft su öffnen. Wenige
hatten Erfolg die Schranke zu passieren
zu der grossen Dämmerung. Grotte, die
vorauscheint. Ich kenne sie, verweilst Du
jemals in den Abgründen suchen sie nach
Deiner Seele und halten sie in ihrer Gewalt.
Höre Mensch, mit vernebeltem Gehirn und
beherzige, meine Warnung; versuche nicht Dich in den
Winkeln zu bewegen, oder Krümmungen, während
der Körper frei ist, hört man das Bellen
der Hunde durchdringend klar und glocken-
gleich, fliehe, wenn Du kannst und ergründe
den Nebel nicht länger!

O puny man, heed ye my warning, seek not
to break open the gate to beyond. Few
there are who have succeeded in passing
the Barrier, to the greater twilit grotto
that shines beyond. For know ye well, that
the dwellers in the Abyss hunt souls like
unto thine to hold in their thrall. Listen O
man of clouded brain and heed ye my warning: move ye not in angles, but curved dimensions, and if while loose from thy body
thou hearest the sound like the bay of hounds
clamoring increasingly through thy being,
retreat, if thou art nimble, to thy body through
cycles and penetrate the veil no more!

Ich kenne alle die
im Licht der erklärten Rechmässigkeit

verweilen, dass andere, die die Schlüssel
und Winkel kennen das Tor geöffnet haben
und für eine Rückkehr ist es zu spät. Ihr
habt den Schlüssel erhalten, aber Eure
Gehirne sind klein und begreifen nicht das
Wort. Deswegen hört den Klang, den
grossen Glockenklang der bellenden Hunde.
Sie sind hartnückig und ausdauernd und
sie kommen durch den grossen, flammenden
Trapezoid ihre Augen glühen mit den
Feuern der Hölle!

Know ye, all who dwell in the light of professed
righteousness, that others who know the keys
and the angles have opened the gate, and
for turning back there is not time. Thou
hast been given the key, but thy minds are
small and grasp not the word. Therefore,
list to the sounds, o ye out there, the great
bell sounds of the baying of the Hounds. They
are gaunt and unquenched, and through the
great blazing Trapezoid they come, their
eyes aglow with the fires of Hell!

Treibewenn du kannst in die Aussmasse
Deine äussersten Bewusstseins und sie
gefangen für immer. Du weisst nichts
über die Grundlage Deiner Schöpfung. Ich
heisse Euch willkommen im Namen Set,
alle werden den Mächtigen Teufel sehen,
die grundlos aushalten in Verzweiflung.
Wir bereiten einen behaglichen Platz um
zu verweilen, über der Qual erhaben.

Drift if ye will, into the dimensions of
your outer consciousness, and be trapped
forever. Ye know not the substance of
your creation. I welcome ye in the name
of Set, all ye who delight in great evil
and sustain thyselves in miseries unfounded.
We prepare a place of comfort for ye to
dwell in torment sublime.

Ringe nicht mit den Affen, die die Tore
der Hölle bewachen, dort liegt das Para-
dies und Anubis ist Wegbereiter.

Wrestle not the apes who guard the gates of
Hell, for there lies Paradise, and Anubis
is the Opener of the Way.

Und wir sprechen mit schlangengleichen
Zungen, dem Bellen der Hunde, dem
grossen glockenklang, der die Schranken
durchbricht—und mächtig sind wir die
regieren, und gering sind die, die leiden.

And we speak with the tongues of serpents,
and the baying of the Hounds, and the great
bell sound that cracks the barrier—and great
are we who rule, and small are ye who suffer.

Der Tag des Kreuzes und des Dreiecks
ist geschaffen. Ein grosses Rad mit
Winkeln in unerkannten Ausmassen,

gerettet für die Kinder der Set, füllt die
Leere und wird zur Sonne am Firmament
der Verachtung!

The day of the cross and the trinity is done.
A great wheel with angles in dimensions unrecognized, save for the children of Set,
fills the void and becomes as the sun in
the Firmament of Wrath!

Proclamation

CELEBRANT:
Siehst Du im Osten das Morgenrot!

See the red sunrise in the East!

Wir wollen die Macht!

We desire Power!

ALL:
Wir werden die Macht haben!

We shall have Power!

CELEBRANT:
Wir wollen das Reichtum!

We desire Wealth!

ALL:
Wir werden das Reichtum haben!

We shall have Wealth!

CELEBRANT:
Wir wollen das Wissen!

We desire Wisdom!

ALL:
Wir werden das Wissen haben!

We shall have Wisdom!

CELEBRANT:
Wir wollen die Annerkennung!

We desire Recognition!

ALL:
Wir werden die Annerkennung haben!

We shall have Recognition!

CELEBRANT:
Wir wollen die Anhänger!

We desire Followers!

ALL:
Wir werden die Anhänger haben!

We shall have Followers!

CELEBRANT:
Was wir wollen, werden wir haben!
Wir werden haben, was wir wollen!

Das Zwielicht ist Hier—
Die Götterdämmerung ist Hier—
Siehst Du im Osten das Morgenrot!
Der Morgen der Magei ist Hier!
Die Welt ist ein-Feuer!
Loki Lebt auf der Erde!

The Twilight is come—
The Twilight of the Gods—
The dawn breaks in the east!
It is the morning of magic!
The world is afire!
Loki lives upon the earth!

Heil, Loki!

Hail, Loki!

Ave, Satanas!

PARTICIPANTS:
Ave Satanas!

CELEBRANT:
Rege Satanas!

PARTICIPANTS:
Rege Satanas!

CELEBRANT:
Heil, Satan!

PARTICIPANTS:
Hail, Satan!

HOMAGE TO TCHORT

How much more precious to man is a small piece of bread than a large ship! But how much money is required for a ship! He that can understand, let him understand.
—Grigory Yefimovitch Rasputin

Few scholars have explored the existence of Devil worship in Russia during the hundreds of years its pagan spirit was in thrall to the Orthodox Church. If questions were asked, the answer was invariably that Russian black magic was either non-existent or a discipline cloaked in Christian euphemism. The latter assumption is, of course, the most accurate.

There is no culture more steeped in dark forces and deities than the Slavonic in general and the Russian in particular. The proportion of Satanic entities in Slavonic mythology far exceeds the usual quota. What is remarkable is that, unlike the *shunned* forces of darkness so often encountered in mythology and religion, Russian devils were regarded with great reverence and/or enjoyment. For this reason, the Christian Church had · a very difficult time fighting the Devil in its Eastern rite. The persistence of Satan, especially among the *muzhiks* (peasants), in the early days of Russian religious orthodoxy required a revamping of the old gods that made Roman Christian transitional techniques pale by comparison.

Unable to banish the old gods of Russia by simply turning them into devils (most were benevolent devils, to begin with), the Christian policy makers supplied their own tailor-

131

made Satan as a sort of catchall evil force. The old Russian gods of wrath and pleasure were relieved of any implements with which they might cause trouble, given innocuous tasks, and assigned a day during which they might be allowed a perfunctory greeting. Some were forcibly "forgotten."

Pyerun, the Formidable One, whose Martian image gave strength and power to those in battle, wielded the thunderbolt by which warriors pledged themselves. His comrade, Volos, the Shaggy One, was the god of the beasts. His snorting stallions and roaring tigers gave inspiration to their two legged brethren. The gentle Christians confiscated Pyerun's chariot and gave him a mill wheel to drag about. His last remaining altar was torn down and thrown into the Dnieper in 988, when Prince Vladimir of Kiev decided to convert to Byzantine Orthodoxy. Volos suffered the indignity of being turned into a barnyard watchman and simple shepherd, and was assigned the new name of St. Vlas.

Volkh, the Werewolf King, was the personification of sorcery, and was called upon by pagan Russians to defend their land in times of need. The *Cult of Kupala* worshipped the magical powers of water. The fern, sacred to the followers of Kupala, like the peacock of the Yezidis, possessed power over riches, beautiful women and wisdom.

The *Cult of Iarilo* refused to die out even as late as the eighteenth century, when the Bishop of Voronezh abolished its practices, which included organized festivities and "Satanic games." Iarilo, the Russian equivalent of Pan, provided fecundity and was particularly honored in spring during the initial sowing.

Zorya, patroness of warriors, rode out on her black horse accompanying Pyerun, and offered protection and invisibility beneath her long veil as it trailed in the wind—the wind provided by Stribog, who was also a wrathful deity.

Though the dualistic principles common to most primitive mythology were present in pre-Christian Russian myths, the dark side (Tchornibog) distinctly predominated. The

White God, Byelobog (not an enemy of the Black God, incidentally; both were considered essential), found greatest favor in White Russia, where his gentle attributes—he guided lost travelers and helped weary peasants with their work in the fields—were welcome.

As was to be expected, the Christians worked overtime to stamp out all such beliefs, thereby placing both the simple *muzhik*, who cherished the good old devils, and the educated, in mortal fear of any remnant of dark forces. Thus a Satanic underground that was carefully cloaked in Christian trappings was bound to develop in Russia. Those who entered such sects were either driven by emotion alone (the followers) or by emotion and reason (the leaders).

By the nineteenth century, religious severity had reached its zenith, with virtually all of Russia adhering to the Orthodox Church. But the Old Gods were preparing a vehicle of retaliation: the men of "God" were revealed, as in other countries, as the real villains, but they were so steeped in their holy self-righteousness, they were unable to imagine their own disintegration. Out of the morass of "goodness" flickered an occasional secular spark of "wickedness." These flickerings kept the Old Ones alive.

Known erotic religious sects existed in Russia during the eighteenth and nineteenth centuries, despite the prevailing Orthodox climate. Evidence indicates they were led and directed by men whose visionary abilities, practices, and goals revealed them as Satanists of the first order. The sect of the *Khlysty* demonstrates this more than any other. Their wise men knew that the passions will always win out. On the surface, the "holy" justification of lust and life provided by the priests of the *Khlysty* seems hypocritical, but it was clearly pragmatic when one understands the religious climate of Russia under the Czars.

The Russian religious response has always been known for overt sensualism, and reversals of emotion. Extravagance in ritual has consistently played a substantial role for Russians.

And the pattern of roaring, drunken debauch followed by contrite and anguished repentence was often outside Western comprehension.

What were the *Khlysty* and from where did they come? They first appeared in Russia about the same time as their antagonistic "separated" brethren, the Skoptsi or "castrators" (circa 1500). Their ritual, though Russian, also contained some foreign adaptation. They celebrated in name and deed such ancient gods and pre-Christian divinities as the Rusalki, and Iarilo, who were the personifications of passion and lust, and the Domovoy, or house *genii*. The *Khlystys* invoked Biblical gods of pleasure, as well as dark, forboding demons like Balaam, and Persian deities like Kors. In the ritual of these "seekers after joy" their whirlings and circumambulations, followed by frenzied sexual release, were virtually indistinguishable from the ecstatic flailing about of the Dervishes.

Undoubtedly the strongest testimony to the influence of foreign sects upon the *Khlysty* was their dogma of "repentance through sin"—the proposition that physical intercourse with a "divine" or chosen one (one in whom a god or the flame of god dwelt) would abolish and transform sin into virtue. This doctrine has overt resemblance to and varies only slightly from one preached by the *Brethren of the Free Spirit* in France, Germany and Czechoslovakia in the fifteenth and sixteenth centuries. *The Brethren of the Free Spirit* was a sect of dissidents that miscarried from the womb of its Mother Roman Church. They taught that within each human being there dwelt a little divine spark (Fünklein). They believed that a simple recognition of this magical essence within each man was enough to liberate one from any restrictions whatsoever, whether social, sexual or intellectual.

The Russian has been, throughout history, predominantly receptive, though sometimes quixotic. And despite the contemporary myth of classlessness, he can easily find his place and remain reconciled to it. Intrigue and change have always hailed from alien spheres. The doctrine of the little flame was, therefore, easily adapted to fit the Russian "soul." Instead of fifty lesser gods of a congregation realizing their divinity, one human leader became divine. To this master, or leader, all bowed with devotion. He was the one who would deliver them from sin! Along with this went the use of a transmogrified Orthodox liturgical format, persistently forming a crosscurrent in the rituals.

Associated with this phenomenon is the Russian Master and convenient villain, Grigori Yefimovich Rasputin, the "Mad Monk" who, through the strength of his personality, and incantations of a rather dubious nature, succeeded in assuaging the hemophilic attacks of the Czarevich, thereupon ingratiating himself into the inner workings of the Czar's court. The *Khlysty* have received much of their notoriety through the supposed association with Rasputin. Though scores of books have been written about him, only one, the perceptive biography by Colin Wilson, seems to paint an accurate picture. If one has sufficient insight, the published memoirs of Rasputin's daughter, Maria, also prove enlightening. The qualities Rasputin possessed will one day become the very stuff from which controlled human greatness will be sought—the sort of greatness that moves man forward in his evolutionary development. In Rasputin some saw that greatness and felt its effect in ways they could not understand, ways that summoned the pain of their own inadequacy. Because he used this inner mechanism, this built-in "inadequacy detector," Rasputin made many enemies, along with many sycophants.

It is significant to note that the persons who brought Rasputin to St. Petersburg and introduced him to court were no mean or feeble occultists, but prominent members of Church aristocracy and urban intelligentsia. Dilettantes and saints (notably, John of Cronstadt) alike hailed him as a holy man with powers from God. (Yet after his death they condemned him as a devil.) Accounts of his *outré* propensities and his powers flourished. It was claimed that a bluish emanation was seen to issue from his lips. He was credited with an uncanny ability to perceive the thoughts and hidden emotions of others. This is borne out by his own words, which also refute the claims of his discreditors who often include thievery among his "vices." His daughter, Maria, recalls him saying, "I never dared to steal or pilfer the smallest thing. I used to believe that everybody would at once see that I had stolen something, since I myself was aware of it as soon as one of my comrades had stolen."

His accomplishments in healing were recognized and widely known, yet not his methods, for Rasputin's was not the usual shamanism of the faith healer. His supposedly extravagant debauchery and libidinous life have been the subject of countless prurient ravings, as has his non-existent role in the *Khlysty* as leader-redemptor of throngs of living bodies. That Rasputin became involved in a political cabal is not to be doubted. He was compelling and outgoing, yet unaffected, in spite of his theatrics, and probably had a high level of natural intelligence. Little is known, however, of the secret meetings held on "special nights" of the year, to which only a few select members, both noble and peasant, were summoned—those evenings that are alluded to but never quite discussed, when Rasputin was "the flame in red" and the "great working" was done.

When Alexandra, the Empress of Russia, was executed in the cellar of the Ipatiev house in 1918, two years after the cruel murder of her *batiuska* Grigori, the guards made a unique discovery. While searching for jewels among her possessions, they found sewn into her bodice a pair of small emerald green dragons given to her by Rasputin many years before. Could he have trafficked with the odd hermetic order which fringed the Russias, *The Green Dragon?* There are also many speculations about the true motivations of the *fin de siècle Khlysty* movement.

Oral communication and fraternal legacy have made the following rite available.

Participants consist of a priest (celebrant), the woman who serves as altar, two acolytes, an illuminator, a gong-striker, and the congregation.

The priest wears a red robe with full sleeves. His assistants are garbed in black robes with red cinctures around the waist. The altar is nude and wears only a metal crown with four lighted candles around its edge. Male congregants wear Russian style tunics over black trousers tucked into black boots. Female congregants wear diaphanous fabric of muted hues, representing the misty veils of the *Rusalki*.

A chained thurible with which to cense the altar and the artifacts is required, as is a large brazier. A small vial of flash powder is placed next to the brazier. The powder is thrown into the brazier according to the rubric. A human arm or leg bone is used as an aspergeant, in honor of *Kashchey*, the skeleton god. All other devices common to Satanic ritual are employed.

The altar sits in a semicircle of ferns, arranged in a fan effect. The chamber is lighted by candles and is decorated in Byzantine motif.

Musical background should be carefully cued to the service, using either Russian folk instruments or suitable recordings. The tiny bells typical of Russian liturgical ceremony should be used wherever appropriate to the rite, and played in the rhythm associated with the *Obikhod*. If in doubt, Modeste Mussorgsky or Walt Disney can be your guides.

HOMAGE TO TCHORT

[The ceremony opens with the purification of the air and benediction of the chamber with the phallus. The chalice is filled, but not presented. The Four Principal Names are invoked to the compass, followed by the calling of the *Third Enochian Key* (from *The Satanic Bible*). The priest (celebrant) then addresses the altar, who is in the "Bast enthroned" (seated upright) position. The priest begins his invocation with arms upraised:]

CELEBRANT:

In the name of he who reigns in the firmament of fire and ice ... arise, ye minions of Tchort the Lord! O mount the blizzards across the steppes and answer to our beckoning! My lips delighteth in Thy praise, O Tchornibog! I am a creature of Thy creation, spawn of Thy flame, craze of Thy mind, carrier of transition! Let comets hail the advent of Thy coming, when we, Thy sons, await on Triglav's heights the omens of Thy will! The glowing coals of ancient sacrifice give birth to spectral shadows who live again as gods of wine and joy!

[Celebrant lowers arms.]

CELEBRANT:

Arise and call the Bones! The living bones upon the Throne!
Slava, Slava yevo silye! Slava!
Kashchei! Kashchei! Immortal man of madness! Slava Tchortu!

PARTICIPANTS:

Kashchei! Kashchei! Slava Tchortu!

CELEBRANT:

Invoke the dancing Goddess, with Pshent of flame. Her yearning knows no bounds; this is Her night to lure the multitudes who sit in judgment of Her lust!
Morena! Morena! Morena! Vyelikaya Mats! Noch eta nasha!

[Congregation performs a metanea (brief bow with right hand lowered to ground), then remains standing. Priest moves to altar and places a kiss upon her body, then steps back and motions for thurible. Acolyte presents thurible to priest, who censes altar first, then congregation. He then returns thurible to acolyte and resumes his invocation:]

CELEBRANT:

Come forth from out the gorge of night! Take flight on leathern wings and soar above the mountain's summit. Cast Thy shadows o'er the earth in answer to our call!
Knyazyam Idut! Dorogu im!

Exaltation

Tchort! Slovye nye abeé myeny!

PARTICIPANTS:
(response)

CELEBRANT:
Balaam! Slovye nye sogliya dayémi!

PARTICIPANTS:
(response)

CELEBRANT:
Pyerun! Seela nye posti zheé maya!

PARTICIPANTS:
(response)

CELEBRANT:
Kors! Mudrostye nye domislí maya!

PARTICIPANTS:
(response)

CELEBRANT:
Dracula! Pravilnoye vos krye syé niye!

PARTICIPANTS:
(response)

CELEBRANT:
Kashchei! Gospodstvo nye eez chét noye!

PARTICIPANTS:
(response)

CELEBRANT:
Iarilo! Tsarstvo nye pobye deé moye!

PARTICIPANTS:
(response)

CELEBRANT:
Sabazios! Krepaste viso cháy shaya!

PARTICIPANTS:
(response)

CELEBRANT:
Morena! Vlastye vyéch naya!

PARTICIPANTS:
(response)

CELEBRANT:
Svarog! Vladichestvo Byeko nyéch noye!

PARTICIPANTS:
(response)

CELEBRANT:
SLAVA TCHORTU!

PARTICIPANTS:
SLAVA TCHORTU!

[Priest receives chalice, places it in front of altar, censes it, and blesses it with the mudra of the flame (closed fingertips of both hands held together, forming an upward point). He raises the chalice to honor the altar, then drains the chalice, which acolyte removes.]

CELEBRANT:

Calling to mind the seekers after joy, who have, at the hands of unnatural and perfidious virtue, perished, we, Thy brothers, ardently desire:
Dominion o'er the teeming lands beneath the darkened sky, above the watery sea!

PARTICIPANTS:

Groznoye Bozhe Tchornava ognia
padai seela!

Dread Lord of the Dark Flame give
power!

CELEBRANT:

Rearing turrets and massive domes with iron walls and courts of stone!

PARTICIPANTS:

Groznoye Bozhe Tchornava ognia
padai krepost!

Dread Lord of the Dark Flame give
strength!

  [Priest receives bone from acolyte, holds it on high, and, facing congregation:]

CELEBRANT:

Thou art a tower of strength and power, and we, Thy brothers, proclaim Thee Lord unto all ages!

[Priest turns to altar, holding bone aloft:]

CELEBRANT:
SLAVA TCHORTU!

PARTICIPANTS:
SLAVA TCHORTU!

[Priest returns bone to acolyte. Other acolyte steps forward and censes priest, who then faces the altar:]

The Self-Glorification

CELEBRANT:
At once I ride upon a sweeping wind, through opalescent skies to the bright place of my desires. I enter hidden worlds through craters in the steppe's great vastness. There, beneath the cringing throngs, midst whirling fife and thundering timpan, the joys of life are mine to taste. There, amidst Rusalkis' languid song, a life of lust is mine to bear; to loll alone in wanton sloth in crimson halls of dissipation . . . for savage man am I!

At once I am removed and feel the reckoning of my twofold completion. My mind is lofty with the enlightenment of Thy creation! My feet are as the mountain's base, firm and one with the house of joy. My eyes are as a pinnacle that views the scattered multitudes of fools who grope for things celestial; who bow and scrape to wan and sallow gods, the spawn of shallow minded men, forsaking life terrestrial while creeping to their graves. I gaze upon the massive hoards that suffocate, like Peter's fish pulled from the lake of life's sweet waters. To perish in Heaven's foul vapors shall be their doom! The fate of fools is justice!

I am the tempter of life that lurks in every breast and belly; a vibrant, torpid cavern, nectar laden, with sweetest pleasures beckoning.

I am a thrusting rod with head of iron, drawing to me myriad nymphs, tumescent in their craving!

I am rampant carnal joy, an agent borne of ecstasy's mad flailing!

Through jagged ice, my father leers with cavernous eyes, below the sphere of earth that is my mother, moist and fertile whore of barbarous delights!

My body is a temple, wherein all demons dwell. A pantheon of flesh am I!

[Priest receives bone from acolyte and places it in an upright position between altar's thighs. Priest performs metanea to altar. Congregation follows suit. The brazier is brought forward and placed before the altar.]

The Greater Litany of Desire

CELEBRANT: (facing brazier)
Great One, hear us now as we invoke Thy blessing:
In the pleasures of the flesh and the tranquility of the mind . . .

ALL:
SUSTAIN US, DARK LORD!

CELEBRANT:

In bold covetousness, desiring all that might be kept with dignity and grace . . .

ALL:

SUSTAIN US, DARK LORD!

CELEBRANT:

In pride in everything we do, display, or are, that shows us not as fools . . .

ALL:

SUSTAIN US, DARK LORD!

CELEBRANT:

For riches yet unclaimed by minds or hands . . .

ALL:

GRANT US, DARK LORD!

CELEBRANT:

For wisdom to be sown in fields which bear great harvest . . .

ALL:

GRANT US, DARK LORD!

CELEBRANT:

For leisure time in pleasure's own pursuit, in which we may all things eschew that speak of vile necessity . . .

ALL:

SUSTAIN US, DARK LORD!

CELEBRANT:

For Thou art a mighty Lord, O Tchort, and unto Thee is all power, honor, and dominion. Let our bright visions be transformed into reality and our works be enduring. For we are kindred spirits, demon brothers, children of earthly joy, who with one voice proclaim:

SO BE IT! SLAVA TCHORTU!

[Priest lifts arms high with fingers spread (incendi):]

CELEBRANT:
Arise, invoke the blasphemous Name
The Lord of Sodom, The God of Cain
Joy to the Flesh forever!

OGON! TY TCHORTU OGONYOK! RAZGORAISA POSKOREI!

[Priest empties powder into brazier, instantaneous to striking of gong, and shouts:]

SABATAN!

[Congregation gives the sign of shunning (hand lifted, palm forward, to shield eyes) and responds:]

PARTICIPANTS:
SABATAN!

[The brazier is removed and the priest moves to altar, hands upraised, and, softly but with great deliberation, repeats the *Exaltation*. The congregation stands in silence. Priest then removes the bone from the altar's lap and steps back from the altar, leaving sufficient room for the congregants to pass before her. All congregants come forward individually, stop before the altar, and bow low. Upon rising, each congregant receives the tip of the bone upon his brow, administered by the priest, who says:]

CELEBRANT:
Ya Tsyebyeh dayu padarok Tchorta. (The gift of Tchort be with you.)

[After the congregation has reassembled, the priest points the bone towards the Sigil of Baphomet and, turning to the congregation, says:]

CELEBRANT:
Forget ye not what was and is to be!
Flesh without sin, world without end!

[The priest closes the ceremony according to the standard procedure.]

PILGRIMS OF THE AGE OF FIRE

> Cependant que persiste
> La splendeur à côté,
> Du plumage bleuté
> De l'orgueil qui s'attriste
> D'un paon jadis vainqueur
> Au jardin du coeur.
> —Verlaine

"Too true, too soon" might be the closing statement of the little band of heretics who survived eight centuries of cruel Christian and Moslem persecution—the Yezidis.

From their mecca—the tomb of their first leader, Sheik Adi—situated on Mount Lalesh near the ancient city of Nineveh, the Yezidi empire stretched in an invisible band approximately three hundred miles wide to the Mediterranean junction of Turkey and Syria on one end, and the mountains of the Caucasus in Russia on the other. At intervals along this strip were seven towers—the Towers of Satan (Ziarahs)—six of them trapezoidal in form, and one, the "center" on Mount Lalesh, shaped like a sharp, fluted point. Each tower was topped by a brilliant heliographic reflector, and was intended to serve as a "power house" from whence a Satanic magician could beam his will to the "descendants of Adam," and influence human events in the outside world.

Like the Watchers—the fallen angels of the Book of Enoch—the Yezidis claimed to be the descendants of Azazel.

The Yezidis believed in a counterpart of the story of Lucifer, i.e. the manifestation of pride banished. Like the legendary lost tribes of Israel, the Yezidis broke away from their roots as a result of unresolved conflicts, and felt a strong justification and purpose because of their unique heritage, which theologically isolated them from all other peoples.

The Yezidis' legend of their origin is no longer fantastic, by scientific standards. It alludes to the creation of the first male and female of the tribe through the principles later set down by Paracelsus for the creation of a homunculus; viz. encapsulation of sperm in a container where it gestates and assumes a human embryonic form.

The Yezidi provided a link between Egypt, Eastern Europe, and Tibet. The language of the Yezidis was Kurdish—similar in sound to Enochian, the language supposedly spoken by the Watchers.

Shortly before Sheik Adi (full name: Saraf ad-Din Abu-l-Fadail, Adi ben Musafir ben Ismael ben Mousa ben Marwan ben Ali-Hassan ben Marwan) died in 1163, he dictated what was to become one of the most legendary manuscripts of all time—the *Al-Jilwah* (revelations). The *Al-Jilwah*, combined with the *Mashaf Res,* which was compiled in the following century, became known as the *Black Book*—the words spoken by Satan to his people. The *Black Book* not only contains the credo of the Yezidi, but their rites as well.

The Yezidis entered their temples through portals bearing the images of a lion, snake, double sided axe, man, comb, scissors, and mirror. The lion represented strength and dominion; the snake, procreation; the axe, potential for good or harm; the man, the god; and the comb, scissors and mirror represented pride. But greater as a symbol of pride, however, was the form taken by Satan in the Yezidi liturgy—the peacock. Because they could not utter the name of Satan (Shaitan) for fear of persecution, the name *Melek Taus* (Peacock King) was used. So great was the risk of outside persecution, that even words that sounded vaguely like the name *Satan* were forbidden.

The vestiges of Yezidi culture that remain today have, as might be expected, met with not only maudlin "understanding" but, worse yet, attempts to whitewash the religion and deny that it was Devil worship. After eight centuries of harming no one, minding their own business, and maintaining the courage of their convictions—despite wholesale massacres of their men, women, and children at the hands of the self-rightous—the Yezidis have finally been granted a sickeningly charitable form of acknowledgment from theologians. It is now patronizingly asserted that the Yezidis were "actually noble and highly moral people," and therefore could *not actually* have worshipped the Devil! It is difficult to assess this as anything other than the most blatant form of selective inattention!

Each time an important Yezidi ritual was to take place, a brazen figure of a peacock (called a *sanjak*) was removed from a secret hiding place by a priest and carried to the temple. It was placed on a pedestal around which a running spring of water played into a small pool. This served as the shrine and icon towards which homage was directed. The water supposedly came from an underground stream which flows through subterranean caverns in a network opening under each Tower of Satan. The point of origin of these streams was thought to be the miraculous well of Islam known as Zamzam. The caverns supposedly terminated at the place of the Masters—Schamballah (Carcosa).

In order to establish proper perspective, in addition to the Yezidis' own beliefs concerning the caverns and the effects of the Towers of Satan, the conjectures of outsiders must be mentioned here. It has long been assumed that the Towers were not limited to the Yezidi geography, but loomed in unrecognized forms in various parts of the world as diverse structures—with each serving as a surface marker for an entrance, allegorical or otherwise, to the nether world. Thus considered, the Yezidi Towers and the Satanic influence they contained become a microcosm of a far more portentous network of control.

The "clans" of the Yezidis consisted of: Sheikan, at Mount Lalesh; Sinjar (Eagle's Lair), in Kurdistan; Halitiyeh, in Turkey; Malliyeh, on the Mediterranean; Sarahdar, in Georgia and Southern Russia; Lepcho, in India and Tibet; and the Kotchar, who, like the Bedouins, moved about with no permanent sector.

The Yezidi interpretation of God was in the purest Satanic tradition. The idea, so prominent in Greek philosophy, that God is an existence absolute and complete in himself, unchangeable, outside of time and space, did not exist in Yezidi theology. Also rejected was the theocratic Judaic concept of Jehovah, and also the Mohammedan God: the absolute ruler. The notion, unique to Christians, that God is Christ-like in character was totally absent. If there was any semblance of a personal manifestation of God, it was through Satan, who instructed and guided the Yezidi toward an understanding of the multifaceted principles of Creation, much like the Platonic idea that the Absolute was itself static and transcendental. This concept of "God" is essentially the position taken by the more highly evolved Satanists. Prayer was forbidden, in the strictest Satanic tradition. Even daily expressions of faith were referred to as "recitals."

Few outsiders had ever penetrated the sanctuaries of the Yezidis. The exceptions have been almost exclusively within the past century when, unfortunately, the sect was waning as an organized movement. Fewer had glimpsed the sacred sanjaks or seen the manuscript of the *Black Book*, for they were carefully guarded from the descendants of Adam, whose progeny had filled the world with mindless clay. Only four texts of the *Black Book* exist, other than the original. One is in Arabic (called the Carshuni text), two are in Syriac (with respective French and Italian translations), and the Church of

Satan's present text, translated from the Arabic manuscript of Daud as-Saig by Isya Joseph.

During the early 1920's writer William Seabrook ventured into the desert and climbed Mount Lalesh, recording his journey (*Adventures in Arabia*) with an objectivity that proved him to be a brave yet compassionate man. At a time when it was literary fashion to trounce the Devil for good measure, regardless of his attributes, Seabrook's affinity for Satan was visible in all his writing as surely as if he had been a Bierce, Shaw, Twain, or Wells. He was one of the few outsiders who, for the first time in the Yezidi history, showed sympathy for their Devil.

By now the Yezidis have largely been absorbed into the world of "those without," but their influence has taken effect. That influence has been manifest, throughout Satanism's underground period, in the procedures of virtually every secret brotherhood since the Knights Templar, and in countless literary works. Now, after the often tragic epic of the Yezidis has become history, it is safe to pronounce the Dread Name.

THE STATEMENT OF SHAITAN
AND WORDLESS RITE OF DEDICATION

The rite begins one hour after sunset.

The congregants enter the chamber and seat themselves on pillows placed on the floor in a semicircle facing the shrine of Melek Taus. The water runs over the rocks surrounding the sanjak and into a pool at their base. Incense burns in braziers at each side of the shrine. The kawwals (musicians) stand against the rear wall of the temple, playing a prelude on flutes, drums, and tambourines. (Note: As emotional response is essential during certain segments of the rite, Europeans and Americans may require music of a modified form. There is much to be recommended in the works of Borodin, Cui, Rimsky-Korsakoff, Ketelbey, Ippolitov-Ivanov, etc., despite the sneers of "purists.")

The priest enters, followed by his assistants, all wearing black robes and red cinctures of braided cord. The priest stands before the shrine, his assistants on either side. The priest's head is shaven. The razor used for this was first washed in the magical waters of Zamzam.

All music stops, and the gong is struck once. The flute resumes playing, very slowly and softly, and the priest invokes the *Third Enochian Key* (from *The Satanic Bible*). When he has finished, the flute stops, and, following a pause, the gong is again struck.

The flute begins to play, as before, and the priest recites from the *Al-Jilwah*, the *Black Book*.

AL-JILWAH

PRIEST:

Before all creation, this revelation was with Melek Tâ'ûs, who sent 'Abd Tâ'ûs to this world that he might separate truth known to his particular people. This was done, first of all, by means of oral tradition, and afterward by means of this book, Al-Jilwah, which the outsiders may neither read nor behold.

(Pause, gong is struck.)

I

I was, am now, and shall have no end. I exercise dominion over all creatures and over the affairs of all who are under the protection of my image. I am ever present to help all who trust in me and call upon me in time of need. There is no place in the universe that knows not my presence. I participate in all the affairs which those who are without call evil because their nature is not such as they approve. Every age has its own manager, who directs affairs according to my decrees. This office is changeable from generation to generation, that the ruler of this world and his chiefs may discharge the duties of their respective offices, every one in his own turn. I allow everyone to follow the dictates of his own nature, but he that opposes me will regret it sorely. No god has a right to interfere in my affairs, and I have made it an imperative rule that everyone shall refrain from worshiping all gods. All the books of those who are without are altered by them, and they have declined from them, although they were written by the prophets and the apostles. That there are interpolations is seen in the fact that each sect endeavors to prove that the others are wrong and to destroy their books. Truth and falsehood are known to me. When temptation comes, I give my covenant to him that trusts in me. Moreover, I give counsel to the skilled directors, for I have appointed them for periods that are known to me. I remember necessary affairs and execute them in due time. I teach and guide those who follow my instruction. If anyone obey me and conform to my commandments, he shall have joy, delight, and comfort.

II

I requite the descendants of Adam, and reward them with various rewards that I alone know. Moreover, power and dominion over all that is on earth, both that which is above and that which is beneath, are in my hand. I do not allow friendly association with other people, nor do I deprive them that are my own and that obey me of anything that is good for them. I place my affairs in the hands of those whom I have tried and who are in accord with my desires. I appear in divers manners to those who are faithful and under my command. I give and take away; I enrich and impoverish; I cause both happiness and misery. I do all this in keeping with the characteristics of each epoch. And none has a right to interfere with my management of affairs. Those who oppose me I afflict with disease; but my own shall not die like the sons of Adam that are without. None shall live in this world longer than the time set by me and if I so desire, I send a person a second or a third time into this world or into some other by the transfer of will.

(Pause, gong is struck.)

III

I lead to the straight path without a revealed book; I direct aright my beloved and my chosen ones by unseen means. All my teachings are easily applicable to all times and all conditions. Now the sons of Adam do not know the state of things that is to come. For this reason they fall into many errors. The beasts of the earth, the birds of heaven, and the fish of the sea are all under the control of my hands. All treasures and hidden things are known to me, and as I desire, I take them from one and bestow them upon another. I reveal my wonders to those who seek them, and in due time my miracles to those who receive them from me. But those who are without are my adversaries, hence they oppose me. Nor do they know that such a course is against their own interests, for might, wealth, and riches are in my hand, and I bestow them upon every worthy descendant of Adam. Thus the government of the world, the transition of generations, and the changes of their directors are determined by me from the beginning.

(Pause, gong is struck.)

IV

I will not give my rights to other gods. I have allowed the creation of four substances, four times, and four corners, because they are necessary things for creatures. The books of Jews, Christians, and Moslems, as of those who are without, accept in a sense, so far as they agree with, and conform to, my statutes. Whatsoever is contrary to these they have altered; do not accept it. Three things are against me, and I hate three things. But those who keep my secrets shall receive the fulfillment of my promises. It is my desire that all my followers shall unite in a bond of unity, lest those who are without prevail against them. Now, then, all ye who have followed my commandments and my teachings, reject all the teachings and sayings of such as are without. I have not taught these teachings, nor do they proceed from me. (Do not mention my name nor my attributes, lest ye regret it; for ye do not know what those who are without may do.) *

(Pause, gong is struck.)

*No longer mandatory

V

O ye that have believed in me, honor my symbol and my image, for they remind you of me. Observe my laws and statutes. Obey my servants and listen to whatever they may dictate to you of the hidden things.

Chand-il-manhatie sobayaka rosh halatie.
Hatna Mesarmen dou jaladie, meskino raba.

My understanding surrounds the truth of things,
And my truth is mixed up in me,
And the truth of my descent is set forth by itself,
And when it was known it was altogether in me.
And all the habitable parts and deserts,
And everything created is under me,
And I am the ruling power preceding all that exists.
And I am he that spoke a true saying,
And I am the just judge and the ruler of the earth.
And I am he that men worship in my glory,
Coming to me and kissing my feet.
And I am he that spread over the heavens their height.
And I am he that cried in the beginning.
And I am he that of myself revealeth all things,
Verily the All-Merciful has assigned unto me names,
The heavenly·throne, and the seat, and the heavens, and the
    earth.
In the secret of my knowledge there is no God but me.
These things are subservient to my power.
O mine enemies, why do you deny me?
O men, deny me not, but submit.
In the day of judgment you will be happy in meeting me.

Who dies in my love, I will cast him
In the midst of Paradise, by my will and pleasure;
But he that dies unmindful of me
Will be thrown into torture in misery and affliction.
I say I am the only one and the exalted;
I create and make rich those whom I will.
Praise it to myself, for all things are by my will,
And the universe is lighted by some of my gifts.

I AM THE KING THAT MAGNIFIES HIMSELF,
AND ALL THE RICHES OF CREATION ARE AT MY
    BIDDING.

I have made known unto you, O people, some of my ways.

So saith Shaitan.

(Pause, gong is struck.)

The priest and his assistants leave the chamber while the kawwals take up their instruments and resume playing.

The congregants remain seated, allowing themselves to absorb the essence of what has been said and the atmosphere which prevails.

Individually, the congregants silently respond to their innermost feelings, not speaking to another.

Each, when his fulfillment has been effected, leaves the chamber as unobtrusively as possible.

THE METAPHYSICS OF LOVECRAFT

Even to his most intimate acquaintances, Howard Phillips Lovecraft (1890–1937) remained frustratingly enigmatic. From the pen of this ingenious New Englander came a collection of the most convincing and thoroughly terrifying works of macabre fiction in modern times. His tales were uniquely embellished with painstaking pseudo-documentation and meticulous description of character and setting. It is frequently said that, once one has read Lovecraft, one disdains the efforts of the competition. This statement has been consistently difficult to refute.

As might be expected, Lovecraft was lionized and extensively imitated by a number of writers whose imaginations were sparked by his celebrated "Cthulhu mythos"—a term commonly given to a series of stories based upon a supernatural pantheon of Lovecraft's own invention. He had a firm conviction that reference to the classical mythologies would undermine the atmosphere of cyclic and spatial disorientation he sought to create. Lovecraft created his own beings, whose prehistoric activities on Earth set in motion the forces of man's civilization and genius, as well as the horrors of his educated imagination. While Freud and Einstein wrestled with their respective disciplines in the isolation of academic specialization, Lovecraft was describing the astonishing influence of physical and geometric law on the psyche. While he might have hesitated to style himself a master of scientific speculation, he is no less deserving of that title than are Asimov and Clarke.

What has puzzled many of Lovecraft's admirers is the author's almost casual attitude towards his work. He repeatedly referred to it as a mere means of financial subsistence. To people who suspected that he entertained a private belief in the mythos, he would reply that an objective detachment from one's material was necessary for effective writing. He was wont to mention the most nightmarish of his narratives with a levity bordering upon scorn, as though he did not consider them of genuine literary substance. As an author, Lovecraft enjoys an established reputation, but what of Lovecraft the philosopher?

Perhaps the most significant clues to the philosophy in the Cthulhu mythos derive from the author's fascination with human history, particularly that of the classical eras. That much of his work used material taken from Egyptian and Arabian legends is well known. There is evidence that he was acutely aware of civilization's effects upon mankind—both educational and repressive. His tales constantly remind the reader that humanity is but a short step from the most depraved and vicious forms of bestiality. He sensed man's drive toward knowledge, even at the risk of sanity. Intellectual excellence, he seemed to say, is achieved in concert with cataclysmic terror —not in avoidance of it.

This theme of a constant interrelationship between the constructive and destructive facets of the human personality is the keystone of the doctrines of Satanism. Theism argues that the integrity of the individual can be increased by a rejection of the carnal and an obedience to morality. Lovecraft recorded his aversion to conventional religious dogma in *The Silver Key*, and he regarded with a similar scorn those who, rejecting religion, succumbed to a controversial substitute, i.e. the popular notion of witchcraft. The concept of worship *per se* is strikingly absent from the Cthulhu mythos. Nyarlathotep, Shub-Niggurath, Yog-Sothoth and Cthulhu are all honored through bizarre festivals, but their relationship to their followers is invariably that of teacher to students. Compare the description of a Lovecraftian ceremony to that of a Christian mass or a

Voodoo rite, and it is clear that the element of servility is definitely lacking in the first.

Lovecraft, like the Miltonian Satan, chose to reign in Hell rather than to serve in Heaven. His creatures are never conclusive stereotypes of good or evil; they vacillate constantly between beneficence and cruelty. They respect knowledge, for which the protagonist of each story abandons every prudent restraint. Critics who consider the Old Ones as Aristotelian elementals—or as a collective influence of malignancy which man must destroy if he is to prevail—suggest a philistine disposition. Lovecraft, if he tolerated such analyses, can hardly have been impressed by them.

Assuming that Lovecraft was an advocate of Satanic amorality, what might have been the content of the ritual observances in Innsmouth, R'lyeh, or Leng? In his work he only goes as far as an occasional lurid line from some "nameless rite" or "unspeakable orgy" celebrated by grotesque apparitions amidst sulphurous caverns of fluorescent, decaying fungi, or against titanic monoliths of disturbing aspect. Perhaps he thought understatement to be more effective in freeing the imaginations of his readers, but clearly, he had been influenced by very real sources. Whether his sources of inspiration were consciously recognized and admitted or were a remarkable "psychic" absorption, one can only speculate. There is no doubt that Lovecraft was aware of rites not quite "nameless," as the allusions in his stories are often *identical* to actual ceremonial procedures and nomenclature, especially to those practiced and advanced around the turn of the last century.

The Innsmouths and Arkhams of Lovecraft have their counterparts in seaside hamlets and forlorn coastal areas all over the world, and one has but to use his senses to spot them: the Land's End sector of San Francisco; Mendocino on the Northern California coast; from the Hamptons to Montauk in New York; between Folkestone and Dover on the English Channel; the Cornish coast west of Exmouth, and numerous points along the coast of Brittany in France. The list is endless. Where men have stood at earth's end contemplating the transition from sea to land with mingled fear and longing in their hearts, the lure of Cthulhu exists. Any offshore oil drilling platform or "Texas tower" is a potential altar to the Spawn of the Watery Abyss.

Lovecraft seems to have correlated the monsters of the canvasses of a hundred Pickmans—the great Symbolist painters of the 1890's—into a twentieth century scenario. His fantasies may well have been a conscious projection of the idea expressed so eloquently by Charles Lamb in his *Witches and Other Night Fears:*

> "Gorgons, and Hydras, and Chimeras may reproduce themselves in the brain of superstition—but they were there before. They are transcripts, types—the archetypes are in us, and eternal."

One cannot help speculating upon a reality suggested by the fantasy—the possibility that the Old Ones are the spectres of a future human mentality. It is as the result of such speculation that *The Ceremony of the Nine Angles* and *The Call to Cthulhu* are presented. One emphasizes potential: the other reflects the dimness of an almost forgotten past. As for the phonetics, they bear no linguistic given name. The translation is as accurate as contemporary methods permit.

CEREMONY OF THE
NINE ANGLES

[This ceremony is to be performed in a closed chamber containing no curved surfaces whatsoever. No open flames are to be in the chamber except for a single brazier or flame pot. General illumination is provided through controlled starlight or moonlight, or via concealed ultraviolet devices. Above and behind the altar platform should appear the outline of a regular trapezoid. The celebrant and participants all wear masks or headpieces to blur or distort the true facial features.

All participants assemble in a half-hexagonal formation facing the large trapezoid emblem. The celebrant stands before the altar, facing the participants. He raises his left hand in the Sign of the Horns:]

CELEBRANT:
N'kgnath ki'q Az-Athoth r'jyarh
wh'fagh zhasa phr-tga nyena phrag-
n'glu.

Let us do honor to Azathoth, without
whose laughter this world should not
be.

181

[*Participants answer the gesture.*]

PARTICIPANTS:
Ki'q Az-Athoth r'jyarh wh'fagh
zhasa phr-tga nyena phragn'glu.

Honor to Azathoth, without whose
laughter this world should not be.

CELEBRANT:
Kzs'nath r'n As-Athoth bril'nwe
sza'g elu'khnar rquorkwe w'ragu
mfancgh' tiim'br vua. Jsnuf a
wrugh kod'rf kpra kybni sprn'aka
ty'knu El-aka gryenn'h krans hu-
ehn.

Azathoth, great center of the cosmos,
let thy flutes sing unto us, lulling
us against the terrors of thy domain.
Thy merriment sustains our fears, and
we rejoice in the World of Horrors in
thy name.

PARTICIPANTS:
Ki'q Az-Athoth r'jyarh wh'fagh
zhasa phr-tga nyena phragn'glu.

Honor to Azathoth, without whose
laughter this world should not be.

[Celebrant lowers hand, then renders the Sign of the Horns with his right hand. All participants echo the gesture.]

CELEBRANT:

N'kgnath ki'q Y'gs-Othoth r'jyarh
fer'gryp'h-nza ke'ru phragn'glu.

Let us do honor to Yog-Sothoth, without whose sign we ourselves should not be.

PARTICIPANTS:

Ki'q Y'gs-Othoth r'jyarh fer-
gryp'h-nza ke'ru phragn'glu.

Honor to Yog-Sothoth, without whose sign we ourselves should not be.

CELEBRANT:

Kh'run-mnu kai Y'gs-Othoth hrn-nji
qua-resvn xha drug'bis pw-nga s'jens
ni'ka quraas-ti kno'g nwreh sbo-j
rgy-namanth El-aka gryenn'h. Ky'rh
han'treh zmah-gron't k'renb phron-
yeh fha'gni y'g zyb'nos vuy-kin'eh
kson wr'g kyno.

Yog-Sothoth, master of dimensions, through thy will are we set upon the World of Horrors. Faceless one, guide us through the night of thy creation, that we may behold the Bond of the Angles and the promise of thy will.

183

PARTICIPANTS:

Ki'q Y'gs-Othoth r'jyarh fer-
gryp'h-nza ke'ru phragn'glu.

Honor to Yog-Sothoth, without whose
sign we ourselves should not be.

[Celebrant raises both arms away from him at a sharp
angle. Participants do likewise.]

CELEBRANT:

Z'j-m'h kh'rn Z'j-m'h kh'r Z'j-
m'h kh rmnu. Kh'rn w'nh nyg hsyh
fha'gnu er'ngi drg-nza knu ky cry-
str'h n'knu. Ou-o nje'y fha'gnu
qurs-ti ngai-kang whro-kng'h rgh-i
szhno zyu-dhron'k po'j nu Cth'n.
I'a ry'gzengrho.

The Daemons are, the Daemons were,
and the Daemons shall be again. They
came, and we are here: they sleep,
and we watch for them. They shall
sleep, and we shall die, but we shall
return through them. We are their
dreams, and they shall awaken. Hail
to the ancient dreams.

PARTICIPANTS:

I'a ry'gzengrho.

Hail to the ancient dreams.

184

[The celebrant now turns to face the altar.]

CELEBRANT:
Kh'rensh n'fha'n-gnh khren-kan'g
N'yra-l'yht-Otp hfy'n chu-si
whr'g zyb'nos thu'nby jne'w nhi
quz-a.

I call now to the unsleeping one, the
black herald, Nyarlathotep, who as-
sureth the bond between the living
and the dead.

PARTICIPANTS:
I'a N'yra-l'yht-Otp.

Hail, Nyarlathotep.

CELEBRANT:
Kh'rengyu az'pyzh rz'e hy'knos
zhri ty'h nzal's za naagha hu'h-
nby jne'w nhi quz-al hjru-crusk'e
dzund dkni-nyeh ryr'ngkain-i
khring's naaghs pyz'rn ry'gzyn
rgy-namanth El-aka gryenn'h tko
f'unga l'zen-zu dsi-r p'ngath
fha'gnu nig-quz'a i'a N'yra-l'yht-
Otp.

O dark one, who rideth the winds of

the Abyss and cryeth the night
gaunts between the living
and the dead, send to us the Old One
of the World of Horrors, whose word
we honor unto the end of the deathless
sleep. Hail, Nyarlathotep.

PARTICIPANTS:
I'a N'yra-l'yht-Otp.

Hail, Nyarlathotep.

CELEBRANT:
I'as urenz-khrgn naaghs z'h hlye
fer-zn cyn. I'as aem'nh ci-cyzb
vyni-weth w'ragn jnusf whrengo
jnusɪ'wi klo zyah zsybh kyn-tal-o
huz-u kyno.

Hail to thee, black prince from the
grotto whose charge we bear. Hail
to thee and to thy fathers, within whose
fane thou laughs and screams in terror and
in merriment, in fear and in ecstasy, in
loneliness and in anger, upon the whim of
thy will.

PARTICIPANTS:
I'a N'yra-l'yht-Otp urz'n naagha.

Hail, Nyarlathotep, prince of the Abyss.

CELEBRANT:
V'hu-ehn n'kgnath fha'gnu n'aem'nh.
Kzren ry'gzyn cyzb-namanth El-aka
gryenn'h kh'renshz k'rahz'nhu
zyb'nos y'goth-e vuy-kin'eh nals
zyh.

In thy name let us behold the father.
Let the Old One who reigneth upon the
World of Horrors come and speak with
us, for we would again strengthen the
bond that liveth within the angles of
the Path of the Left.

[The celebrant stands directly before the altar, clenching
both fists and crossing the left hand over the right against
his chest.]

CELEBRANT:
I'a Sh'b-N'ygr'th aem'nh El-aka
gryenn'h. I'a aem'nh kyl-d zhem'n.
I'a zhem'nfni n'quz n'fha'n-gn ki-
qua hu-ehn zyb'nos.

Hail, Shub-Niggurath, father of the
World of Horrors. Hail, father of the
hornless ones. Hail, ram of the Sun
and deathless one, who sleepest not
while we honor thy name and thy bond.

PARTICIPANTS:
I'a Sh'b-N'ygr'th.

Hail, Shub-Niggurath.

[The Goat of a Thousand Young appears. All participants clench their fists after the fashion of the celebrant.]

CELEBRANT:
I'a aem'nh.

Hail, father.

PARTICIPANTS:
I'a aem'nh.

Hail, father.

SHUB-NIGGURATH:
Phragn'ka phragn. V'vuy-kin'e f'ungn
kyl-d zhem'n k'fungn zyb'nos Z'j-m'h
kyns el-kran'u. F'ungnu'h zyb-kai
zyb'nos rohz vuy-kh'yn.

I am that I am. Through the angles I
speak with the hornless ones, and I
pledge anew the bond of the Daemons,
through whose will this world is come
to be. Let us speak the Bond of the
Nine Angles.

CELEBRANT AND PARTICIPANTS:
I'a aemn'h urz'vuy-kin w'hren'j
El-aka gryenn'h. F'ung'hn-kai
zyb'nos rohz vuy-kh'yn n'kye
w'ragh zh'sza hrn-nji qua-resvn
k'ng naagha zhem v'mhneg-alz.

Hail, father and lord of the angles, master of the World of Horrors. We speak the Bond of the Nine Angles to the honor of the flutes of the laughing one, the master of dimensions, the herald of the barrier, and the Goat of a Thousand Young.

ALL:
V'ty'h vuy-kn el-ukh'nar ci-wragh zh'sza w'ragnh ks'zy d'syn.

From the First Angle is the infinite, wherein the laughing one doth cry and the flutes wail unto the ending of time.

V'quy'h vuy-kn hrn-nji hyl zaan-i vyk d'phron'h El-aka gryenn'h v'jnus-fyh whreng'n.

From the Second Angle is the master who doth order the planes and the angles, and who hath conceived the World of Horrors in its terror and glory.

V'kresn vuy-kn k'nga d'phron'g kr-a El-aka gryenn'h p'nseb quer-hga phragn uk-khron ty'h-qu'kre vuy-kin'e rohz.

From the Third Angle is the messenger,

who hath created thy power to behold
the master of the World of Horrors,
who giveth to thee substance of being
and the knowledge of the Nine Angles.

V'huy vuy-kn zhem'nfi d'psy'h
dy-tr'gyu El-aka gryenn'h f'ungn-
ei si'n si-r'a s'alk d'hu'h-uye
rohz.

From the Fourth Angle is the ram of
the Sun, who brought thy selves to be,
who endureth upon the World of Horrors
and proclaimeth the time that was, the
time that is, and the time that shall be;
and whose name is the brilliance of
the Nine Angles.

V'cvye vuy-kn kh'ren-i kyl-d
zhem'n lyz-naa mnaa r'cvyev'y-kre
Z'j-m'h gryn-h'y d'yn'khe cyvaal'k
h'y-cvy-rohz.

From the Fifth Angle are the hornless
ones, who raise the temple of the five
trihedrons unto the Daemons of creation,
whose seal is at once four and five and
nine.

V'quar'n vuy-kn fha'gn Z'j-m'h
ki-dyus dyn-jn'ash cvy-knu ukr'n
hy-rohz.

From the Sixth Angle is the sleep of
the Daemons in symmetry, which doth
vanquish the five but shall not prevail
against the four and the nine.

V'try'v vuy-kn djn'sh dys-u n'fha'g-
nir Z'j-m'h r'n hy-kre'snvy'k kr'n-
quar.

From the Seventh Angle is the ruin
of symmetry and the awakening of the
Daemons, for the four and the nine
shall prevail against the six.

V'nyr vuy-kn hrn-njir vu'a lyz-naa
mnaa r'nyrv'y Z'j-m'h gry-h'y d'yn-
khe cyvaal'k h'y-cvy-rohz.

From the Eighth Angle are the Masters
of the Realm, who raise the temple of
the eight trihedrons unto the Daemons
of creation, whose seal is at once four
and five and nine.

V'rohz vuy-kn i'inkh-v zy-d'syn
ur'bre-el hy'j whreng'n nakhreng'h
yh'whreng'n kyenn'h.

From the Ninth Angle is the flame of
the beginning and ending of dimensions,
which blazeth in brilliance and darkness
unto the glory of desire.

SHUB-NIGGURATH:

K'fung'n zyb'nos Z'j-m'h kyns el-
gryn'hy.

I pledge the bond of the Daemons,
through whose will this world hath
come to be.

CELEBRANT AND PARTICIPANTS:

Ki'q zyb'nos k'El-aka gryenn'h.

We honor the bond upon the World of
Horrors.

SHUB-NIGGURATH:

Ki-iq kyl-d zhem'n.

Hail to the hornless ones.

CELEBRANT AND PARTICIPANTS:

Ki-iq Sh'b-N'ygr'th aem'nh El-aka
gryenn'h.

Hail to Shub-Niggurath, father of the
World of Horrors.

SHUB-NIGGURATH:

Zhar-v zy-d'syn.

Unto the beginning and the ending
of dimensions.

CELEBRANT:
Zhar-v zy-d'syn.

Unto the beginning and the ending
of dimensions.

[The Goat of a Thousand Young no longer appears. The
celebrant faces the participants.]

CELEBRANT:
Ty'h nzal's kra naaghs n'ghlasj
zsyn'e ty'h nzal's za'je oth'e
kyl-d zhem'n f'ungh'n. Nal Y'gs-
Othoth krell N'yra-l'yht-Otp.
I'a Y'gs-Othoth. I'a N'yra-l'yht-
Otp.

The gaunts are loose upon the wold,
and we shall not pass; but the time
shall come when the gaunts will bow
before us, and man shall speak with
the tongues of the hornless ones. The
way is Yog-Sothoth, and the key is
Nyarlathotep. Hail, Yog-Sothoth. Hail,
Nyarlathotep.

PARTICIPANTS:
I'a Y'gs-Othoth. I'a N'yra-l'yht-
Otp. I'a S'ha-t'n.

Hail, Yog-Sothoth. Hail, Nyarlathotep.
Hail, Satan.

THE CALL TO CTHULHU

[This ceremony is to be performed in a secluded location near a major body of water—a large river, lake, or ocean. The ideal site for the proceedings would be a natural stone cavern at the water's edge, but a grove of trees or a concealed inlet will serve.

The ceremony must take place at night, preferably at a time when the sky is heavily overcast and the water is tempestuous. No special articles of attire—such as robes—or decorative paraphernalia are to be used. The single exception is that all participants must wear the medallion that bears the Seal of Satan: it may be dangerous to disregard this provision.

A large bonfire is kindled. The celebrant—who will assume the presence of Cthulhu—stands above and apart from the participants, holding aloft a torch which has been treated to yield a blackish-blue glare. The celebrant is not present at the beginning of the ceremony.

All participants light the bonfire and assemble in a jagged circle about it. Their eyes are directed toward the blaze for the duration of the ceremony.]

PRINCIPAL PARTICIPANT:
My brothers and sisters of the ancient blood, we are gathered to pronounce the Call to Cthulhu. I cry again the word of the

Abyss—that great void of the dark waters and shrieking winds where we lived in ages past. Hear the deathless ones, and say with me the call to the Eternal Serpent who sleeps that we may live.

ALL:

Ph'nglui mglw'nafh Cthulhu R'lyeh wgah'nagl fhtagn.

PRINCIPAL PARTICIPANT:

I'a k'nark Cthulhu kyr'w qu'ra cylth drehm'n El-ak. U'gnyal kraayn: (Hail, great Cthulhu, who art known to all races of the deep ones who walk upon and beneath the earth. Hear thy honored names:)

ALL:

KRAKEN — POSEIDEN — SABAZIOS — TYPHON — DAGON — SETHEH — NEPTUNE — LEVIA-THAN — MIDGARD — CTHULHU! Ph'nglui mglw'nafh Cthulhu R'lyeh wgah'nagl fhtagn. I'a Cthulhu.

[The figure of Cthulhu appears.]

CELEBRANT:

Ph'reng-na Y'gth El-aka gryenn'h w'yal'h-ji kyr dy-tral's k'heh.

PARTICIPANTS:

From Yuggoth I am come to the World of Horrors, here to abide and to rule for all eternity.

CELEBRANT:

V'kresn vuy-kn grany'h arksh ty'h nzal's naaghs wh'rag-ngla oth'e tryn-yal El-aka gryenn'h.

PARTICIPANTS:

Through the Third Angle I journeyed, casting forth the jackals of time and singing with the men who gamboled upon the World of Horrors.

CELEBRANT:

Yal'h-el kh'rgs-th'e w'raghs-tryn'h gh'naa-w'ragnhi. R'nkal ngh'-na ka-ii gh'na-nafh fhtag's.

PARTICIPANTS:

I walked upon the earth, and I taught the men to laugh and to play, to slay and to scream. And for them I died not, but for myself I died and have slept.

CELEBRANT:

W'ragh zh'sza kz'yelh naa-g naaghs hu-glyzz jag'h gh'an cyve vuy-k'nh v'quar.

PARTICIPANTS:

The flutes of the laughing one shriek through the chasms of the Abyss, and the darkness boils with the perishing of the five angles in the sixth.

CELEBRANT:

Y'trynh na'gh'l w'raghno'th vR'lyeh ngh'na fhtagn-w'gah kr'hyl zaan-i vyk'n.

PARTICIPANTS:

I danced and killed, and I laughed with the men, and in R'lyeh I died to sleep the dreams of the master of the planes and the angles.

CELEBRANT:

M'khagn w'ragnhzy dys-n'gha k'dys-n'ghals k'fungn-akel zaht'h k'halrn ghr-kha n'fhtagn-gha.

PARTICIPANTS:

Hear me, for I cry the end of the god of death, and of the god of dying, and I speak of the laws of life that you may reject the curse of the death without sleep.

CELEBRANT:

K'aemn'h kh'rn K'aemn'h kh'r Kaemn'h kh'rmnu. N'ghan-ka fhtagni-kar'n gha'l. V'naa-glyz-zai v'naa-glyz-zn'a cylth.

PARTICIPANTS:

The Old Ones were, the Old Ones are, and the Old Ones shall be again. I am dead, but I sleep and am therefore not dead. From the depths of the waters I come, and from the depths the deep ones also have come.

CELEBRANT:

V'szel kh'ra-fhtagn k'bahl'dys-n'gha yga'h-h'j n'fhtag'h z'aht. V'glyzz k'fungn cylth-a v'el cylth-Cthulhu k'fungn'i.

PARTICIPANTS:

For ages you also have slept through the reign of the god of death, and now you have awakened to life. From the sea I call to the deep ones, and from the earth the deep ones call to Cthulhu.

CELEBRANT:

N'kys ka-naaghs v'prh-gh'nya k'K'aemn'h az'zl-inkh'v naaghs k'zhem'nfi k'zhe-t'h ur-geyl n'el k'fungn i-inkh'v k'nga y'ilth-kai.

PARTICIPANTS:

Forget neither the abyss of origin, nor the Old Ones who brought to you the flame of the Abyss, nor the ram of the Sun, nor the Eternal Serpent who raised you upon the earth and delivered to you the flame from the messenger.

CELEBRANT:

P'garn'h v'glyzz. (Go now from the sea.)

[The celebrant casts the torch into the bonfire. He retreats to the darkness.]

CELEBRANT:

Vuy-kin'e glyz-naaghs y'kh'rain k'r'heyl vuy-kin'el s'nargh's cylth. (The angles of the watery Abyss are no more, but other angles there are for the deep ones to command.)

PARTICIPANTS:

V'yn'khe rohz v'schm'h v'ragsh kyr-reng'ka w'nath-al y'keld v'fnaghn K'aemn'hi. I'a Cthulhu! I'a S'ha-t'n! (By the Seal of Nine and by the Shining Trapezoid, let none hazard thy wrath, for we are known to the Old Ones. Hail, Cthulhu! Hail, Satan!)

THE SATANIC BAPTISMS

Since the formation of the Church of Satan, many persons wishing to solemnize their newly acknowledged dedication to Satanic principles have requested a "baptismal" rite, whereby they might utilize an established form of religious observance for more compatible beliefs. As a result, two distinct ceremonies have been created, one for infants and the other for adults who have reached the legal age of consent.

Of course any ceremony performed for an infant is not really performed for the child, but for the parents. With this thought in mind, a baptism in the traditional sense could serve no productive purpose by Satanic standards. A child's "baptism" according to Satanic tenets must, therefore, be in the nature of a celebration, rather than a purification. In this sense, a Satanic "baptism" for children becomes a Christian baptism in reverse. Instead of cleansing the infant of "original sin" and preparing him for a life of blind devotion to an existing faith, the Satanic "baptism" pays homage to the miracle of the child's creation, his capacity for unbefouled development and his freedom from hypocrisy.

The children's ceremony included here is intended for children under the age of four; beyond that age ideas alien to Satanic development have been absorbed into the child's mind, via the formal teachings of older and often unwiser humans. Once that process has begun, only the individual can thereafter rightfully choose a credo for himself and formalize it. Hence, the need for a Satanic "baptismal" rite for adults.

"Legal age of consent" is essential to the adult's ceremony, because of the double-edged sword that term provides. Environmental legislation contends—rightly or otherwise—that when a person reaches a certain chronological age he is capable of managing his own affairs and making his own decisions. It is assumed that any such decisions are a by-product of his mental and emotional development, the result of both heredity and environment. This behavioral composite is also influenced by what is referred to as "proper guidance" or "improper guidance," depending upon who is speaking. Attainment of legal age enables one to "misguide" himself as he sees fit, and to assume the blame or take the credit for his own actions.

Inasmuch as all Satanists would be considered "misguided" by the pious, we have no wish to offend further the sensibilities of the self-righteous by luring apple-cheeked boys and girls into "unholy rites and unspeakable orgies." Virtually every unsuccessful (usually deservedly so) contemporary sect or cult which has deviated from established Christian dogma has fallen because the pious majority has been outraged by said cult's traffic with underaged persons. Admittedly, many of these cults have been little more than confidence games, or sexual outlets, cloaked in white-light spirituality. While we concur that age is no proof of sound judgment, we recognize the importance of working within the legal framework of society.

There is nothing inherently wrong with morality: in fact it is necessary for the great enjoyment which comes with controlled, rational, and harmless immorality. What *is* objectionable, though, is a morality based on obsolete and exhausted principles. The children's "baptism" set forth here rejoices in the infant's intrinsic freedom from such expendable principles. The adult's baptism celebrates the individual's rejection of those precepts and his subsequent adherence to Satanic ethic.

What, it will be asked, will young readers, whose ages fall between the two baptisms, do to commit themselves to Satanism? The answer is that whether you are right or wrong, your beliefs will not be held valid by those outside unless money can be made on them. If enough of you believe in the principles of Satanism, they will find ways of making money on your faith. Then, without realizing it, they will have contributed to Lucifer's rise by making popular what once was shunned as evil. Your faith in Satanism need not be formalized by baptism in order to work its magic. Your faith need only be outspokenly stated. That is what you can do.

THE SATANIC "BAPTISM"
Adult Rite

Participants include: the priest or acting priest, the initiate(s), any assistants who may be required by the priest, and other selected witnesses present by invitation of the initiate, but whose presence is not a prerequisite for the performance of this ceremony.

Accouterments are all those standard to Satanic Ritual as described in *The Satanic Bible*, plus a receptacle with earth and one with sea water, and a brazier and charcoal, and incense. Participants are appareled in the customary manner, i.e. black ceremonial robes and (except for priest) peaked, full-faced hoods, and amulets bearing the Symbol of Baphomet. The ceremony commences with the initiate barefoot, robed in white, wearing no undergarments. An additional black robe and Baphomet amulet will be needed for the initiate later in the ceremony and therefore should be prepared and placed nearby.

Before formally entering the chamber, participants don appropriate vestments, arrange artifacts and implements conveniently but without sacrifice of magical correctitude: the brazier, the initiate's chair or stool, and the receptacles containing soil and sea water are placed near altar. Light the altar candles and the candle to be used by the priest during the ceremony (Black Flame), ignite charcoal, and complete all other preparations. Then begin appropriate music.

Upon entering the chamber, the priest (or celebrant acting in that capacity) assumes his position before the altar. The initiate and the other participants stand to either side, with the priest's assistants positioned as their respective roles require. Preliminary functions of ritual are performed in customary order. The initiate is then called forward and kneels before the priest, who recites the *First Enochian Key* (from *The Satanic Bible*) and proceeds to address the initiate.

PRIEST:

In the majestic light of undefiled wisdom, awake and enter into the Arcadian Wood wherein all thy lingering falsehoods shall be as dead bark, stripped from thy trunk: where thy futile hypocrisies, known and unknown, shall no longer envelop thee in mind and body.

Cast off thy white robe of lies and confront thy Prince, revealed as thee once began life, undraped and unashamed. Thou mayest breathe again that first breath now as night winds freshen from the far reaches of Belial.

[Initiate arises, disrobes, and sits in the chair provided, his feet supported by a footstool. Celebrant passes flame of candle four times under soles of initiate's feet. As he does so, he speaks:]

PRIEST:

Through this, the Black Flame of Satan, thou walketh in Hell. Thy senses are awakened to the joy of rebirth. The Gates are flung wide and thy passage is heralded by the deathless cries of His guardian beasts. His searing brand shall be evermore emblazoned on thy consciousness: its fiery meaning shall make thee free.

[Priest gestures with his hands in recognition of the Air of Enlightenment as he pours incense into brazier. He intones:]

PRIEST:
We bring of Thy Garden, O Mighty Lucifer, the fragrances which abound therein. Vapors of millennia which Thou hast shared with Thy chosen flock are rekindled now to fill this chamber with Thy presence. We toll the bell in Thy name and thereby summon the whispering voices of wonder from all the regions of Thine Empire.

Breathe of His breath, O brother of the night, and nourish thy yearning brain.

From the despair and agony of thy former direction, thy new path is tonight set forth in all the brilliance of Lucifer's flame. His zephyrs now guide thy steps into the ultimate power which knowledge brings. The blood of those who fail is eternally bright on the jaws of Death, and the hounds of night pursue their hapless quarry relentlessly.

They who walk amongst us who bear deceit: verily they shall perish in blindness. Turn thy back on the vile and despise them: follow the Black Flame to unending beauty in mind and body.

[Priest removes some earth from container and, while pressing the soil back and forth against the initiate's soles and palms, speaks:]

PRIEST:

Now, as before, when the Mother of us all cushioned our paths with the pure pagan silt of ages, She offers Herself anew. As thy true role of Earth-child emerges and pervades thy being, return for this and all time thy feet to Her bosom. Revel in the shimmering glow from the hearth of thy heart, and make thy pact of devotion with all Her children whose paws have tracked and learned the way of Belial. Seek and be glad, for infinity speaks only to those of self-realization, who know, and hear, and heed The Law.

[Priest anoints the initiate with water from the sea, and speaks:]

PRIEST:

From the arid wastes and bleaching bones and nothingness thou cometh into our midst. With parched and swollen lips, with ears thirsting for words of truth, thy quest has led thee to the shrouded and misty subterranean caves of Leviathan.

It is from this brine that all life springs forth. Within thee flows remnant saline seas, maintaining thy kinship with the denizens of the deep, nameless creatures of Dagon who, borne upon eternal tides, shall sustain thee as they have sustained their land dwelling brethren in aeons past. Take comfort in thy briny heritage.

Arise now, and wrap thyself in the mantle of darkness, wherein all secrets abide.

[Initiate stands and dons the black robe. Priest then places amulet around initiate's neck, while saying:]

211

PRIEST:

I place the amulet of Baphomet upon you, and therewith seal thy eternal commitment to Satan, Lord of thy chosen realm, and thy unyielding loyalty to the wondrous order of His creation.

Raise thy right hand in the Sign of the Horns and receive this, thine oath:
Thou, who have forsworn the divine mindlessness, do proclaim the majesty of thine own being amongst the marvels of the universe. Thou rejecteth oblivion of self, and accepteth the pleasure and pain of unique existence. Thou art returned from death to life, and declareth thy friendship with Lucifer, Lord of Light, who is exalted as Satan. Thou receiveth the Sigil of Baphomet and embraceth the black flame of cherished enlightenment. Thou hath assumed this Infernal commitment of thine own volition, without let or hindrance: this act being done without coercion and of thine own desire and according to thy will.

[Priest faces initiate and, with sword in hand, describes with its point an inverted pentagram. It is traced in the air directly in front of the initiate's chest and the newly consecrated amulet. Priest and initiate face altar and present the Sign of the Horns.]

PRIEST:
Hail, Satan!

Initiate:
Hail, Satan!

[Priest tolls bell: Pollutionary. He then extinguishes black flame, and intones:]

PRIEST:
So it is done.

THE SATANIC "BAPTISM"
Children's Ceremony

To Zeena and Orwell

Participants consist of a priest, an assistant, the child who is to be glorified, and the child's parents. Other congregants may be present at the invitation of the child's parents.

Black robes are worn by all participants except the child, who wears a bright red gown with open-faced hood. The talisman of Satan is suspended by a chain or ribbon worn around the neck on the outside of the red gown. The child is seated (or lain, if a very young infant) upon the altar platform before the symbol of Satan, depicted on the west wall of the chamber.

In addition to the accouterments standard to Satanic Ritual (see *The Satanic Bible*), earth and sea water, and an appropriate receptacle for each, will be needed. It should be noted that incense is *not* employed in this rite. The use of incense is so firmly entrenched in secular religious procedure—an aspect of life not yet known to the child—that establishing such an identification with Satanic rite in the child's mind is unmagical. Though adults seem to require it, children don't. If scents are to be present within the chamber, they should be odors for which the child has displayed favorable or elated response, such as chocolate, warm milk, or other favorite food, an animal pet, etc.

Background music must be carefully selected, as small children are epicurean in their choice of tonalities. The author has found that the themes of Edvaard Grieg's "Hall of the Mountain King" and Gabriel Pierné's "Entrance of the Little Fauns," when played at a slow and even tempo, are ideal.

Archaic English (thee, thy, etc.) has been eliminated from this rite because of the possibility of confusion to the child, for it is reasonable to assume he is unaccustomed to such verbiage at the age of his taking the rite. If the child's parents are made happier by archaic usage, substitutions can be made.

The priest stands directly in front of the altar, his assistant to his left, and the child's parents to his right. The ceremony is begun in the standard manner. The priest reads the *First Enochian Key* (from *The Satanic Bible*), then proceeds with the glorification:

PRIEST:
In the name of Satan, Lucifer, Belial, Leviathan, and all the demons, named and nameless, walkers in the velvet darkness, harken to us, O dim and shadowy things, wraith-like, twisted, half-seen creatures, glimpsed beyond the foggy veil of time and spaceless night. Draw near, attend us on this night of fledgling sovereignty. Welcome a new and worthy sister (brother), (child's name) , creature of ecstatic, magic light. Join us in our welcome. With us say: welcome to you, child of joy, sweet passion's daughter (son), product of the dark and musk filled night, ecstasy's delight. Welcome to you, sorceress (sorcerer), most natural and true magician. Your tiny hands have strength to pull the crumbling vaults of spurious heavens down, and from their shards erect a monument to your own sweet indulgence. Your honesty entitles you to well-deserved dominion o'er a world filled with frightened, cowering men.

[The acolyte hands a lighted black candle to the priest,

who passes the flame four times under the child's feet, saying:]

PRIEST:

In the name of Satan, we set your feet upon the Left-Hand Path. Four times above the flame you pass, to kindle lust and passion in your heart, that the heat and brightness of Schamballah's flame may warm you, that your feelings and emotions may burn bright and passionate, to work your magic as you wish.   (name)   , we call you, as your name gleams forth within the flame.

[The priest returns the candle to the acolyte, who then presents the priest with the bell. The priest rings the bell softly about the child, intoning:]

PRIEST:

In the name of Lucifer, we ring about you, brightening the air with sounds of tinkling wisdom. As your eyes receive enlighten-ment, so shall your ears perceive the truth, and separate life's patterns, that your place will be found. We call your name into the night: O hear sweet   (name)'s   magic name.

[Returning the bell to the acolyte, the priest is given the earth jar. He removes a small amount of earth and lightly rubs it against the child's hands and feet (palms and soles), saying:]

PRIEST:

In the name of Belial, we place His mark upon you, to solemnize and etch in memory the dark, moist planet—the Pit from whence you came—the jetting stream of manhood fertilizing Mother Earth. Thus was it always and to time's end will it be. _____(name)_____, we call you, that your power, too, may last unending, always strong as man and earth, for they are one with thee.

[Returning the earth jar, the priest takes up the vessel of sea water and anoints the child's hands and feet, saying:]

PRIEST:

In the name of Leviathan, and with the great salt sea, we dress your being in the substance of creation. May all the dwellers in the watery abyss smile upon you, _____(name)_____, and swirl about you lovingly. May the oceans surge an anthem to your glory, O little spawn of briny heritage.

[The priest returns the vessel to the acolyte and, taking up the sword, places its tip upon the child's brow, saying:]

PRIEST:

By all the images set forth for childhood's fancy, by all things that creep and shuffle through the faerie fane of night, by all the silken rustles on the wind and croakings in the dark, O frogs and toads and rats and crows and cats and dogs and bats and whales and all you kith and kin of little ones like she (he) who rests before you: bless her (him), sustain her (him), for she (he) is of that which needs no purification, for she (he), like all of you, is perfection in what she (he) is, and the mind that dwells within this head is moved by *your* god, the Lord of IS, the All-Powerful Manifestation of Satan.

[The priest lifts the sword from the child's forehead and, as part of the same gesture, raises its tip up to the Sigil of Baphomet, above and behind the child. All others present face the altar and lift their right arms in the Sign of the Horns.]

PRIEST:
HAIL, _____ (name) _____ !

ALL OTHERS:
HAIL, _____ (name) _____ !

PRIEST:
HAIL, SATAN!

ALL OTHERS:
HAIL, SATAN!

[The ceremony is concluded in the usual manner.]

THE UNKNOWN KNOWN

Despite others' attempts to identify a certain number with Satan, it will be known that Nine is His number. Nine is the number of the Ego, for it always returns to itself. No matter what is done through the most complex multiplication of Nine by any other number, in the final equation nine alone will stand forth.

The true ages of time are cast in the likeness of Nine, with all cycles obedient to its Law. All matters of terrestrial concern may be evaluated by the infallible resolution of Nine and its offspring. Action and reaction relative to humanity's tribal needs are contained within successive nine-year periods: the total of both (eighteen years) is called a Working. The beginning and end of each Working is called a Working Year, and each midway point between the Working Years displays a zenith of intensity for the Working which has been brought about.

Nine eighteen-year Workings equal an Era (162 years). Nine Eras equal an Age (1,458 years), which has been mistakenly called a millennium. Nine Ages equal an Epoch (13,122 years).

Each Age (1,458 years) alternates as Fire or Ice, each differing in the means by which the Control presents its dictum. During an Age of Ice, man is taught to refrain from his pride and to retreat from himself; then he will be good. During an Age of Fire, man is taught to indulge himself and to tear himself open and look inside; then he will be good. During an Ice Age, God is above. During a Fire Age, God is beneath. Throughout each Age, big things occur each eighteen years, for the Control must maintain a cycle of action and reaction within the greater cycle of Fire and Ice.

Meaningful and portentous messages are cast forth each eighteen years, and are acted upon for the eighteen years which follow, at the end of which a new statement appears. The Ice Age from which we recently emerged began in the year 508 "A.D." Just as the zenith of passion for what each Working has inspired occurs halfway between the Working Years, so the greatest intensity of each Age's message occurs at its midpoint. Thus in the year 1237 "A.D." man's fervor for what the last Ice Age represented had reached its summit. That Age ended in 1966, and the new Age of Fire was born.

The twentieth century has prepared us for the future and the coming of the Age of Fire was well heralded in the last Working Years of the Ice Age. The peoples of the Earth have been touched by the vehicles of 1894, 1912, 1930, and 1948, and communication has been well wrought. The new Satanic Age was born in 1966, and that is why His Church was built.

The infant is learning to walk, and by the first Working Year of his age—that is to say 1984—he will have steadied his steps, and by the next—2002—he will have attained maturity, and his reign will be filled with wisdom, reason and delight.

REGE SATANAS!
AVE, SATANAS!
HAIL, SATAN!